Scandinavian

Folk Patterns

for Counted Thread
Embroidery

Scandinavian

Folk Patterns

for Counted Thread Embroidery

by Claudia Riiff Finseth

Pacific Search Press

For Rick
and his wonderful support
For Dad
and my Scandinavian heritage
For Mom
who taught me to appreciate all heritages

Pacific Search Press
222 Dexter Avenue North,
     Seattle, Washington 98109
©1987 by Claudia Riiff Finseth. All rights reserved
©1987 designs, patterns, and illustrations by
     Claudia Riiff Finseth
Printed in Hong Kong

Edited by Margaret Foster-Finan
Designed by Judy Petry
Color photographs by Ben Erickson and Mark
     Bush.

Library of Congress Cataloging-in-Publication Data

Finseth, Claudia Riiff.
     Scandinavian folk patterns for counted thread
embroidery.

     Bibliography: p.
     Includes index.
     1. Counted thread embroidery—Scandinavia—
Patterns. 2. Decoration and ornament—Scandinavia.
I. Title. TT778.C65F56   1987   746.44   87-9111
ISBN 0-931397-21-9
ISBN 0-931397-20-0 (pbk.)

Contents

Acknowledgments

If I had known from the outset how long it would take to write this book or how many people it would involve, I am sure I would have been overwhelmed and immediately put the idea out of my mind as impractical. But the whole thing evolved over several years, from a small project into a bigger and bigger one, always surprising me by the dimensions it was taking on. Little by little, more and more people got involved in my work. Now, in looking back, I see a network of experts and supporters who together helped me build *Scandinavian Folk Patterns*. To these people I am deeply grateful:

Gloria Pederson, proprietor of Gloria's Scandinavian Gift Shop in Parkland, Washington, whose enthusiasm about my designs was the original spark for this book, and who, together with her husband, Arne, opened her shop inventory to me as a form of financial support for the project.

Paul Porter, graphic artist, who patiently taught me to make first-rate graphics.

Megan Benton, Deanna Dally, Ellie Long, Linda Parrish, Suzanne Rahn, and Marcia Sherry, my critics, editors, and sources of inspiration, ideas, and support.

Hilma Attoniemi, Nina Bertelsen, Asta Cox, Steve Melton, Kerstin Ringdall, Berit Ringo, Dorothy Tobiason, and Auden Toven, who shared memories of Scandinavia with me, translated research, and verified my text for accuracy.

Vilavanh Bounthysavath, Mary Donahue, my mother-in-law, Ruth Finseth, Tracy Frietas, Denette Laufmann, Karin LaFollette, Ellie Long, Kynda Nordstrom, Jilene Nicholson, Linda Parrish, Cathy and Marta Swenson, and especially Marcia Sherry and my mother, Marguerite Riiff, who helped me put in the over 150,000 stitches that make up the examples of the designs. Janice Burwash and Kristine Isaacson, who sewed baskets and little girls' jumpers.

Mary Hansen, Wera Wilhelm, and many others in The Needle Arts Guild of Puget Sound, who graciously shared their expertise with me.

Katie Earll and Bob Mead of Art Concepts Gallery in Tacoma for frame designs that complement and enhance the needlework.

Ben Erickson and Mark Bush, excellent photographers.

The Scandinavian museum curators who helped me with my research and provided photographs from their museums' collections.

The people at Pacific Search Press—great people to work with—and especially Carolyn Threadgill, who believed in my work and challenged me to present it to the best of my ability.

My parents, who often watched their grandchildren while I was immersed in research and writing.

My husband, Rick, a real partner in life, who proofreads my work, helps raise the children, and keeps the house in some semblance of order, all while carrying on his own career.

And finally, I feel a special sense of gratefulness to my children, Eric and Sarah. Being at home with them has allowed me the chance to be creative.

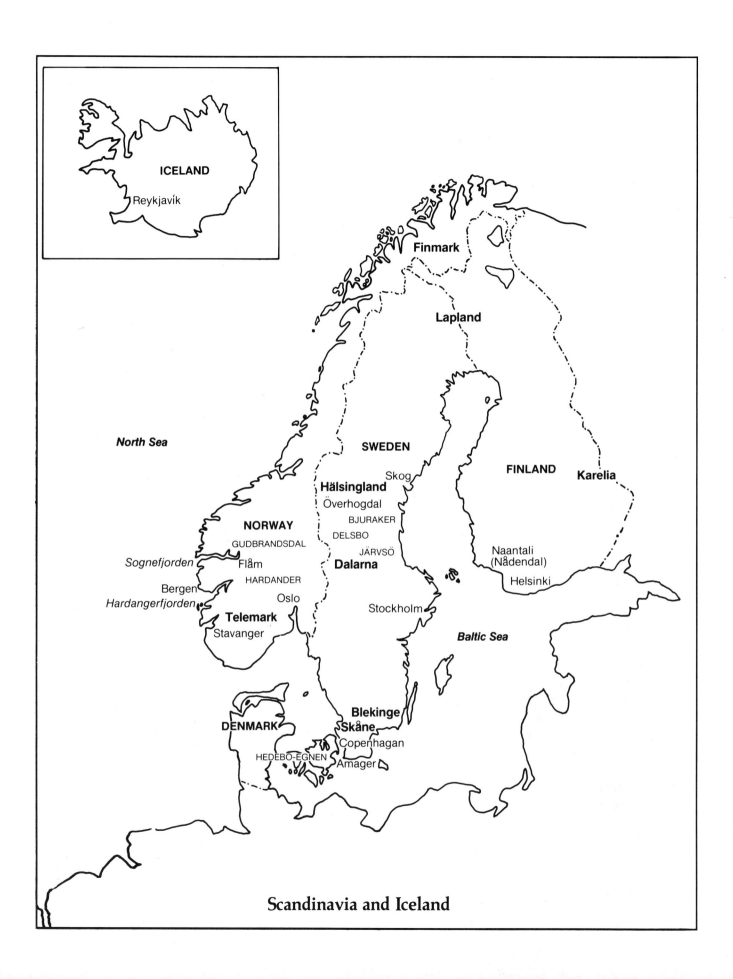

ICELAND

Reykjavík

North Sea

Finmark

Lapland

SWEDEN

Skog

FINLAND

Karelia

Hälsingland

Överhogdal

BJURAKER

NORWAY

DELSBO

GUDBRANDSDAL

JÄRVSÖ

Naantali
(Nådendal)

Sognefjorden

Flåm

Dalarna

Helsinki

Bergen

HARDANDER

Hardangerfjorden

Oslo

Telemark

Stockholm

Stavanger

Baltic Sea

Blekinge

DENMARK

Skåne

Copenhagan

HEDEBO-EGNEN

Amager

Scandinavia and Iceland

Introduction

As Soothing as an Old Folk Song

After that [after Sigurd died] Gudrun went away into the forest and heard on all sides the howling of wolves, and she thought she would be happier if she could die. She went on until she came to the hall of King Hálf, where she stayed with Thóra, Hakon's daughter, for seven half-years in Denmark, having been greeted there with great welcome. There she wove a tapestry and wrought upon it many great deeds and fair sport, as was frequent in those times—swords and byrnies and all kinds of kings' trappings, and King Sigmund's ships as they sailed out from land. And she wove also there the fight of Sigar and Siggeir in the south at Fjon. Such was their pleasure, Gudrun and Thóra, and Gudrun got some comfort from her grief.

"The Völsung Saga"
Iceland, circa A.D. 1400

In counted thread embroidery you begin by finding the center: the center of the pattern, then the center of the material. The stitching begins at that center, and from there the image emerges, moving out with a rhythm that follows the pattern. Sometimes the picture unfolds in circular form like a slow blooming flower or circlets of water in a pool, and sometimes it grows before you like the sun rising on the horizon. But the rhythm and the growth cannot take place without that first act of centering. Centering sets up the balance in the beginning, so that in the end there is sufficient cloth on all sides for the piece to be whole and complete. In this way needlework is a replica of life, for the goal in life is also to find our center and, in so doing, grow toward wholeness.

Embroidery—and all handcrafts—not only duplicates the process of achieving balance in our lives, it helps us attain it. The old Scandinavian embroiderers had a saying about counted thread, that it was "soothing as an old folk song." Simple, rhythmic, and patterned, counted thread can be an avenue to peace or regeneration or invigoration.

Through the simple rhythm of counted thread, we can empty ourselves of other stimuli and attain the silence in which we finally hear our own inner voice. We cut through the bombarding world, to the heart of the matter. We can find the center, and in so doing, a wellspring for problem solving, meditation, and prayer. Counted thread embroidery can in this way become a form of liturgy—a silent liturgy through which we meet our inner voice. As we stitch, suddenly an answer to some struggle we have had may be there. Resolution. It is not a conscious process, not anything logical or sequential; the answer is simply within us, waiting for us to hear it.

It is not magical. And it is not new to us. As babies we had to find our sense of balance before we could sit, crawl, walk, run, or dance. Often, along the way to adulthood, we lose contact with all we originally learned about balance; what we can explain by reason and logic becomes all that we will accept as truth, while anything else is suspect as primitive or mystical. In the process we lose valuable coping aids, such as the picture weaving was for the grieving Gudrun, who had just lost her husband, Sigurd. We are like a sea of icebergs, acknowledging only a small part of ourselves and our potential. In reviving handcrafts such as needlework, we can reach beyond logic. We can begin to restore our sense of balance.

All craftspeople understand that handcrafts offer us the chance to create, and creativity itself is a marvelous, freeing, beneficial force. Creating with our own hands is satisfying; it seems to fulfill a deep need in us. And handcrafts give us a new view of creation. Embroidery can deepen our sense of the seasons, not just through seasonal patterns, but through the materials themselves. One way that I know winter is coming is when I want to work with warm wools, and when I want to put the wool away and get out the cool cotton or linen, then spring is close by.

Color and its counterpart, texture, unfold in my hands as I stitch—sometimes even as they are blossoming in my garden—and I marvel at the miracle they are and the pleasure they bring. Shades of blue, red, yellow, brown, cranberry, teal, and sage can please the eye in an almost palpable way. There is a palette to the touch as well: smooth, rough, fine, coarse, fuzzy, silky—all to be felt and enjoyed. Many of my embroiderer friends prefer not to use hoops or frames, because they love feeling the cloth in their hands. The materials exude a spirit of their own; they change and soften as one works with them. Canvas is stiff like cardboard to begin with, but in the end it is nearly as soft as cloth.

There is creativity in each of us. No one is without this very human ability, although some of us have as yet to discover a creative channel that best suits us. The idea of carrying on a folk tradition may be intriguing, but not all folk arts are readily accessible. Counted thread embroidery is accessible; with a tapestry needle, the only essential tool, any of the stitches can be learned in minutes. Even those unfamiliar with textile arts can quickly become adept at counted thread and create lovely heirlooms. Creating with those we love in mind gives us added inspiration. With the long life of embroidery materials, there is no reason why we cannot stitch not only for the next generation, but for many generations more.

I have long had an interest in Scandinavian folk arts. It began with a little wooden box that was given to me when I was a child. The box was from Norway and had been my grandmother's. Since then I have come to appreciate the qualities of Scandinavian folk art and to respect the craftspeople whose work has survived the centuries. I have been influenced not only by the old embroidery and textiles, but by the carving, the painting, and most especially, by the folk literature; these have been my inspiration.

My goal with this book has been to present something new based on this long and great folk art tradition. With words, I have tried to embroider a picture of how the counted thread embroidery tradition in Scandinavia was birthed and grew, changed and evolved, waxed and waned, all with a wonderful living spirit of its own.

How were embroidery and other folk arts integrated into the Scandinavian peasant life? For them it was not just pretty, it was serviceable; not made just for the results, but to experience the process as well. It was part of their vocation of living off the land, and it was a way in which they experienced the seasons. We have lost much of this process of integration, but not irretrievably. Through this book, I have endeavored to regain it. By connecting the history and folk traditions of Scandinavian counted thread with embroidery today, I have attempted to build a bridge between then and now.

If *Scandinavian Folk Patterns* brings an added dimension to your embroidery, then my goal will have been reached. I hope that embroidering will give you these benefits: a relaxing, peaceful rhythm; a means of hearing your inner voice; the deep satisfaction of creating; delight in color and texture; a new appreciation of Scandinavian folk art; and a legacy of beautiful heirlooms. When embroidering the designs in this book, I hope the knowledge of the history and traditions behind them will add to their meaning and beauty for you.

Claudia Riiff Finseth
March 1987

Chapter One

The Scandinavian Tradition of Narrative Textiles

She [Brynhild] knew more skills than other women: she laid a tapestry with gold and embroidered on it the great deeds that Sigurd had done—the slaying of the dragon, the taking of the treasure, and the death of Regin. Now a day or so after her return, it is told that Sigurd went riding in the forest with his hounds and hawks and many retainers, and when he came back, his hawk flew up to a high tower and settled down by a window. Sigurd went after his hawk. There in the tower he saw a beautiful woman whom he recognized as Brynhild. It appeared to him that both were equally fair, her beauty and the tapestry on which she was working. . . .

"The Völsung Saga"
Iceland, circa A.D. 1400

From their beginning the textile arts of Scandinavia have shared visions of power and fantasy and a deep understanding of the language of symbols, making the old textiles timeless. They were beautiful when they were first made, and those that survive are so striking now that they take the breath away and will always feel ancient and unfathomable and beautiful beyond reckoning.

Some of these old narrative textiles of Scandinavia tell about political events, some about beliefs, some about personal matters, but all tell us things we might not otherwise know about early Scandinavia, for there was no written language there until the coming of Christianity in the Middle Ages. So it is largely through handcrafts that the first Scandinavians told their stories: through picture stones, carvings, and the narratives of weavings and embroideries.

I define embroidery here in its broadest sense, as any textile work done with needles or sticks, while weaving is worked on a loom. Picture weaving is related to both, in that it is done by moving a bobbin by hand through the warp threads on a loom—a form of darning. More technically, weaving is the making of fabric, while

embroidery is a way of embellishing an already existing piece of cloth, or of making decorative trim for cloth. Counted thread is only one of several kinds of embroidery including free embroidery, laid and couched work, drawn thread work, huck-weave, and various kinds of lace making such as tatting, knot work, and *sprang*.

The oldest surviving Scandinavian narrative textiles date from Viking times (A.D. 800–1050). Perhaps earlier ones existed, but they have not survived weather and time. The majority of earlier embroideries and weavings all appear to be of natural brown wool with no figures, such as the oldest known Scandinavian embroidery, the three-thousand-year-old Borum Eshöj hair net, which was found in a Bronze Age burial mound. The net, skillfully made in a technique called *sprang*—a form of braiding with sticks—was placed over the hair of a Danish noblewoman by those who prepared her body for burial.

From cloth fragments we can see that dyes were not commonly used until the early Migrations (A.D. 200–500). It is from then that we find the first quantities of blue, red, and yellow all-wool fabric. Linen fragments date only as early as the last half of the Migrations (A.D. 500–800), which was about the time the nomadic Scandinavian tribes began to settle and cultivate the land for such crops as flax. Settlement also meant a chance to develop more sophisticated looms and other textile equipment as well as techniques.

The Viking Age was a fascinating and violent epoch in history, and the Vikings recorded what was in their conscious and unconscious in powerful artistic images, including narrative textiles. Most Viking embroidery was also preserved in graves on burial clothes. It is usually wool thread stitched on wool cloth, often in symmetrical motifs of two birds or animals facing each other across a central plant or tree—Yggdrasil, the world tree, the center of the Norse mythological universe. The embroiderers spun their wool in the ancient method of distaff and spindle: they clumped the raw wool on a distaff tucked in the belt, pulled out a wisp and twisted it into yarn, then wound it on the spindle. Local plants provided a variety of dyes:

tree barks produced tans; lichens gave browns and yellow; the roots of the madder or Northern bedstraw plant gave a red dye par excellence, turning cloth various shades of orange-red; vied and woad dyes were blue. More colors were produced by mixing dyes, such as blue and yellow to make green.

The Öseberg Cloths

The significance of color for Scandinavians is evident in early Viking artifacts. Seeds of the vied plant were found in the graceful Öseberg Viking ship, unearthed near Oslo at the turn of this century. This ship was meant as transportation to the world of the dead for a Viking queen, Asa, daughter of King Harald Redbeard and wife-by-force to King Gudröd the Magnificent of Vestfold, who killed her father and brother to obtain her. Asa was a true Viking at heart; she eventually got

A piece of the Öseberg picture weavings, A.D. *850. Note the lady in the passenger seat. (Courtesy Universitetet i Oslo Oldsaksamlingen)*

revenge by having a servant kill her husband one night after he had had too much to drink. She then reigned alone until her death in about A.D. 850. "And the men spoke of how commanding the woman was," one skald writes of her.[1] The vied seeds were placed in her grave to accompany her to the other world, where it was important that she be able to dye her textiles when she set up household.

Asa must have been a woman who appreciated art, for her ship-grave was full of some of the most magnificent handcraft artifacts of any Viking find. Not least beautiful are the textiles: fragile fragments of wool and linen picture weavings and silk embroideries that were bundled together to accompany Asa on her nether-bound ship. These long, slender Öseberg linens, now dim and crumbled, once adorned the walls of a royal hall, reflecting scenes of contemporary life. In their original yellow, red, and black on ecru they must have been eye-catching.

In one scene, Viking figures parade from right to left as if on some busy thoroughfare. Prancing horses draw wagons much like the real carved wooden wagon found with the ship. On the textile in a passenger cart rides what appears to be a dignified, even haughty noblewoman—perhaps Queen Asa herself. Pedestrians, most carrying spears (it was a sign of the times that few left home without their weapons) and wearing a wide-legged style of trousers under tunics, fill the spaces between rows of horses and wagons.

Another part of the weaving depicts a cavalry formation of warriors, replete with shields. They are borne by proud horses with magnificently decorated harnesses, braided manes, and knotted tails. The formation is precise. The careful grooming of the horses tells us they were highly valued and beloved by Viking peoples.

A very grim scene of the tapestry shows great twisted sacrificial trees with corpses hanging from their limbs. This is Norse mythology: the cult of Odin, the god who hanged himself from a tree to gain powers of prophesy and knowledge, and who was worshipped in turn with sacrifices of hanged

victims. The Valkyries, the three handmaidens of Odin, float above the sacrifices.

Textiles and Early Literature

As ancient textiles tell us of Norse life, so Norse literature, which had its beginnings in the twelfth century, reveals much about the uses and significance of textiles in Viking times. Red and blue, the rarest colors in Viking textiles and perhaps the most treasured, foreshadow dramatic events in literature. For instance, heroes from the sagas often wear a blue cape when they have an important deed to do. Odin, the god of death, always wears a blue cloak to meet the fallen warriors after battle and lead them to Valhalla.

Early Norse writings also mention long, narrow picture tapestries like those of Öseberg. Ninety feet was not an unheard-of length for such textile works. Literature describes the festive use of these tapestries, hung to cover great ancient halls such as Herot, where Beowulf battled the monster Grendel.

Norse history and literature reveal that cloth was so valuable that it was often used as currency, valued relative to silver. At one point in Gisli's Saga, Gisli is paid "360 ells of homespun and some silver." Vikings were quite happy to be paid in cloth, which in the cold north was nearly as essential to their survival as food.

The Viking Age came about to some extent because of the repressiveness of the early kings of Norway. This was particularly true of the first man to unify Norway, Harald Fairhair, who ruthlessly and violently fought his way from ruler of a small district in eastern Norway to dominion over the whole country in the year A.D. 872—all because, his saga says, a maiden refused him as husband until he could "claim Norway as his own and be sole king over it as is King Gorm in Denmark and Eirík in Uppsala."

"She has reminded me," said he [Harald],

"of what it seems strange that I never thought of before." And still further he said, "I make this vow . . . that I shall neither cut nor comb my hair before I have conquered all of Norway, with all its taxes and revenues, and govern it altogether, or else die." His marshall, Guthorm, thanked him much for these words and said it was a royal task to fulfil his vow. ("The Saga of Harald Fairhair," *Heimskringla*, Snorri Sturlusson, Iceland, thirteenth century)

And fulfill his vows Harald Fairhair did. As a result, many of those who opposed him were forced to leave Norway. Homeless and outlawed they searched for lands and, on invading them, fought for control with the local inhabitants. Before the discovery of Iceland, Vikings overtook parts of the British Isles. Others steered their ships south along the continental coast and down inland rivers, and by A.D. 911 they had taken Normandy in the north of what is now France. Ironically, a century and a half later, the descendents of these two groups of Vikings set to war against each other; in 1066 the Normans, under their duke, William, invaded and conquered England. The story of this conquest is told in the Bayeux tapestry.

The Bayeux Tapestry

Over 230 feet long and only twenty inches high, the Bayeux tapestry is the longest embroidery from the ancient Western world. It is worked in laid and couched stitches (which make a solid figure) and stem and outline stitches, very similar in style and technique to later Icelandic and Norwegian works. On a bleached linen background, the wools are colored in the rich, muted tones that only natural dyes can give: shades of rusts, blues, greens, and mustard.

The first scenes on the tapestry, moving from left to right, show the English nobleman Harold swearing fealty to William again and again during the time when Edward the Confessor, the heirless king of England, was dying. The tapestry then illustrates Edward's death and how Harold, rather than keeping his oaths to William, suddenly claims the crown for himself. The betrayed William builds a fleet of Viking-style ships and sails his soldiers and their mounts to England, where in the Battle of Hastings they defeat Harold. The embroiderers depict the battle with amazing intensity and detail. The linen is covered with charging horses bearing soldiers in chain mail: swords, battle-axes, and spears in full thrust. Several fallen soldiers lie upon the ground. Battle horses tumble as only hard-charging steeds can.

The Bayeux tapestry tells the story of William and Harold's conflict from William's very Norse point of view. The Norse Code was one of the honor of the oath; one's word was truth, and a promise made between two people was a contract. If that word was broken, as Harold broke his to William, then the only honorable recourse was revenge. As the Norsemen saw it, William had no choice but to invade England and challenge Harold, and this is the way the Bayeux designers present the story in wool.

The origins of the Bayeux tapestry are uncertain, but it was probably sewn in Normandy or England in the century after the conquest. What is undisputed about the work is that it is Scandinavian: its way of thought and artistry, although 150 years removed from its homeland, is still essentially Norse. [2] In fact, the Bayeux tapestry is similar enough to the Öseberg textiles to be considered their descendant—a step further in the evolution of Scandinavian story textiles. Their handsome, curve-necked horses and primitive figures are strikingly akin even though each is dressed in the fashion of their time.

Other Early Narrative Textiles

A thirteenth-century weaving and an embroidery fragment, found in the medieval churches of Överhogdal and Skog, Sweden, share

The Bayeux tapestry: Harold claiming the throne of England for himself. (By authorization of the city of Bayeux, France)

the spirit of the Öseberg and Bayeux works. The figures have the same primeval feel, as if they are nearly as old as the world itself, or as if they spring from the wells of human memory. The Överhogdal tapestry's horses and deer run through the threads like Stone Age petroglyphs. The long, narrow Skog hanging depicts animals, horsemen, standing humans, and most interestingly, a steepled church— one of the first symbols of Christianity in Norse textiles. This embroidery is thought by some to represent the struggle between paganism and Christianity, but perhaps it is as much the story of the meshing of the two; old meets new and out of that meeting comes something different yet. The old Scandinavian stave churches may have had crosses on the inside, but carved dragons often guard them from the doorposts. The Skog hanging

is the mood of the time laid out for posterity on cloth.[3]

The Coming of Christianity

The coming of Christianity in the early Middle Ages brought new inspiration to Scandinavian handcrafts, and as embroiderers had decorated their great halls with their work, so now they also adorned their churches. Walls, altars, chalices, and priests were draped in the finest embroidery, sometimes accented with threads of precious metals, for parishes took pride in making their churches as beautiful and rich as possible.

The cross and the crucifixion became the new

A scene of tumbling battle horses, from the Bayeux tapestry. In the Battle of Hastings, William defeated Harold. (By authorization of the city of Bayeux, France)

subject matter became outdated, first when Christianity became common, and then when the Reformation deposed the saints. Many older textiles were cut up and used for backing of newer works. Indeed, even in fairly recent history—during the French Revolution—the Bayeux tapestry was nearly used as a wagon cover before it was rescued by a person who understood its significance.

The medieval textiles that did survive often did so because they were put away, usually under the church floor, and then forgotten. Subsequent generations did not know they existed until by chance, perhaps hundreds of years later, someone happened to take up the floor. Such is the case

An embroidered wall hanging from Skog Church in Hälsingland, Sweden, A.D. 1050–1200. (Statens Historiska Museum, Stockholm)

dominant themes for embroiderers. Yggdrasil, the world tree, evolved into the vine and the branches as old symbolism was reborn into Christian iconography. Yet these new works looked very similar to the more ancient ones, for the Scandinavians depicted their new faith with the same dramatic simplicity that pervades their pagan works. The altar frontal from Hals church in northern Iceland, which depicts the crucifixion, and the Norwegian Høyland Church frieze of the three Wise Men are two of the finest early examples of this.

Few textiles survive from the early Middle Ages in Scandinavia, and most that do are ecclesiastical. Certainly many more were made, but a lot of them may have been destroyed because their

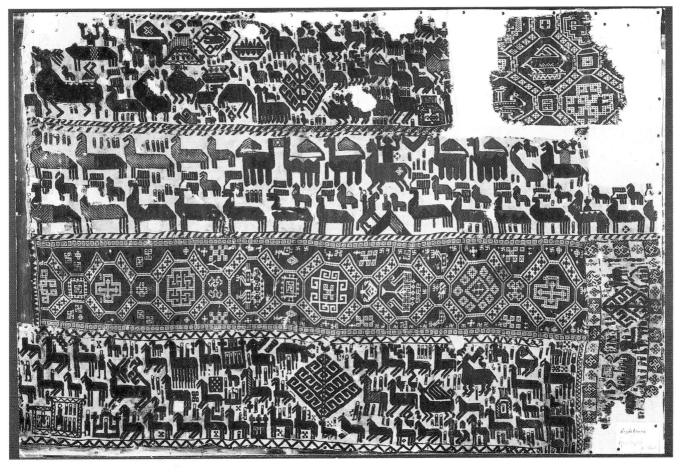

The Överhogdal tapestry in Swedish double weave from Härjedalen province, Middle Ages. (Jämtlands Läns Museum, Östersund, Sweden)

with a late twelfth-century Norwegian weaving depicting the Labors of the Months, which was a popular theme in the Middle Ages. It was found under the wooden floor of Baldishol Church when it was seven hundred years old.

The Reformation in Scandinavia was fairly peaceful. This was probably because Christianity arrived relatively late, and Catholicism did not have long to become deeply rooted; by 1550 all of the state churches were Lutheran. Almost simultaneously textiles began to take on Biblical themes, as though they were reflecting the times. And while the stories were as old as that of Adam and Eve, the mood was contemporary; even the three Wise Men and the Wise and Foolish Virgins

sport ruffled Elizabethan collars.

It seems like a strange mix, but history is not linear, it is spiral and convoluted, and the past is always somehow pertinent to the present, and the present an equation of the past plus more. The old Scandinavian narrative textiles record history for us in these kinds of living terms—fluid, as it was happening, without the hindsight that assigns everything to a specific decade (the kind of consideration that would put the Wise Men in first-century Eastern dress only). It is with a sense of story rather than analysis, a striving for art as much as an attempt to record history, that the handcrafters of the old narrative textiles wove and embroidered. They succeed in telling us more

Altar frontal (1617) from Háls Church, northern Iceland. Long-armed cross-stitch in wool on linen. (National Museum of Iceland, Reykjavik. Gisli Gestsson, photographer.)

Norwegian Biblical picture weaving of the Wise and Foolish Virgins in sixteenth-century dress. (Norsk Folkemuseum)

about history than simple facts could. These old textiles carry us through the ages: faith and fashion come and go in wool; kingdoms rise and fall on linen; life is recorded by nimble hands. The very heart of the land seems soaked into the cloths, pulsing at us even as we look at them hundreds of years later.

Chapter Two

Counted Thread and the Common Folk

A broidered cloth   of fine bleached linen
Did Mother take   covered the table.
Loaves of thin bread   light, made of wheat
She then carried in   laid them down on the cloth.

Then she brought trenchers   filled to the brim,
Plated with silver   put them on the table,
Meat well browned   and fully cooked birds.
There was wine in a crock   bright were the goblets.
They drank and chatted.   Thus passed the day.

"Rigsthula," *The Poetic Edda*
Iceland, fourteenth century

It is Christmas Eve in Scandinavia in the year 1800. You dance a shiver as you stomp the snow off your shoes on the threshold of the storage building. Your cold hands fumble with the ring of keys as you try to unlock the carved door. Inside it is just as cold and dark, but the smell of grain greets you, and that sweet aroma reminds you of the summers when you sit in here and weave.

In the corner are the chests of linens. You emptied most of them yesterday to decorate the house, all but one last bundle. By the dim light coming through the door that stands ajar, you open the pine chest and, with an eager anticipation reach down to lift out the bundle wrapped in old homespun rags. Then, leaving and locking the door behind you, you cross the icy, sparkling snow that crunches softly beneath your feet and walk back to the main house of big, dark logs, to the warmth of its fireplace, and the pungent fragrance of fresh pine clippings carpeting the floor. The straw goat your husband made for Yule grins at you from the corner.

Turning up the kerosene lamp, you unwrap the bundle on the pine plank table. Inside are three pieces of a fine bleached linen table set embroidered in red cross-stitch—a gift left to you when Aunt Sigrid died last year.

As you take up the tablecloth and feel the smooth, crisp linen, you savor the rich texture of it between your thumb and fingers. Unfolding it, you flick it and send it billowing over the pine planks. Then you carefully spread the bright red runner across the middle of the cloth. The fibers of the linen acquire a sheen and suppleness with age, as if it thrives on use. Even the faded stains from past holidays do not detract from its loveliness.

Aunt Sigrid bought the linen bolt from a southern Scandinavian peddler. It was a rare purchase, because farmwives make most of their own linen. But Aunt Sigrid had wanted to remake the old family tablecloth and could not resist the fine fabric, which was an especially good buy because the flax harvests had been plentiful that year, and linen was in abundance. Aunt Sigrid spun the embroidery thread herself from her best flax and dyed it with madder for a bright orange-red.

She then copied the old tablecloth, which had been in the family more than four generations and patched and repaired until that was no longer feasible. Counting the little stitches one by one, she reproduced the zigzags, leafy flowers, and eight-point stars of the original cloth on her new linen, careful of exact detail. When she was done, she had enough cloth left to make a table runner and shelf border. These she embroidered in the same red linen thread, making fanciful figures and birds.

Ah! The Christmas feasts from your childhood that were spread upon these cloths! Not only was there the usual dried reindeer meat, boiled potatoes, flatbreads, salmon and herring and cod, but special treats of sour cream porridge or rice pudding, pork from the pig slaughtered especially for Christmas, and the rich delicacies cooked one by one on irons and in molds.

You look around your house and realize that it looks much like Aunt Sigrid's did in your childhood. Large white linen hangings cover the ceiling. They billow over you from rafter to rafter, meeting the tops of the walls with braided fringe. More hangings cascade down the walls to the built-in benches. Some are embroidered and some are woven designs: blue figures parade here, red motifs dance there. They fill your dark house with color and warmth and light: the festive air made visible.

After feasting at Aunt Sigrid's, everyone would gather around the crackling fire to tell folktales and snatches of old sagas, and Bible stories. Sometimes, as the teller spoke, you would look around the room and recognize the story on one of the hangings. Perhaps it was the Ten Wise and Foolish Virgins floating blue on a cloud of white on the ceiling; or Sigurd the Dragonslayer on his great steed Grani; or the forest of a folktale, curling in vines so intricate it became a puzzle to solve. Enchanted animals drew you in until you were riding great white bears, fabulous reindeer, and magnificent round horses while you lay fast asleep on a bench or in your mother's lap. In the morning you woke to find yourself in one of Aunt Sigrid's wall beds, cozy between sisters and cousins under piles of coverlets and furs.

But goodness! Where has the time gone? You lay the red cross-stitch shelf border and give it a smoothing. Tonight will be a good time to tell your own children the story of the linen table set. Perhaps one will ask to have it passed on to them. There! It looks like Christmas now, and just in time, for you hear the sound of sleigh bells nearing.

In being a part of this scene you can imagine the difference between the past and the present. For between that Christmas Eve of 1800, which was in the midst of the great era of district and regional folk art in Scandinavia, and our time lies the chasm of the Industrial Revolution.

During the centuries of district and regional art, roughly the years 1700–1850, handcrafts were practiced in every peasant home in Scandinavia, and the results were of both cultural and social significance. The handcrafts were important, and ability in them was respected. The place held by counted thread and textile arts in general during this time and their development and prominence in each facet of Scandinavian life is worth exploration.

The Beginnings of Counted Thread Embroidery

Counted thread embroidery seems to have originated in the near East or the Mediterranean area and probably came up the trade routes with merchants and returning travelers. It became popular in Germany and England at least a hundred years before it took hold in Scandinavia, but once it came to the far north, around the year 1500, it quickly spread to all of the Scandinavian countries.

At that time navneklude, literally "name rags," or what we call samplers, became part of the training for young Danish schoolgirls. It soon followed in other areas as well. On these the girls cross-stitched the alphabet, their name and age, and perhaps some figures or designs and borders. This was the way they learned their letters. The sampler was often graded; its handiwork was one proof of whether its maker was capable of running a household. Later on, when making linens for her own home, a young girl could use her sampler alphabet as a pattern for monogramming towels, shirts, and other linens. Borders from the sampler could be copied onto tablecloths, curtains, and skirt hems.

Most early Scandinavian samplers were typical of those all over Europe, for the designs came mostly from German or English pattern books, available as a result of the printing press. At first samplers were sewn only in towns, where children

A peasant sampler made in 1780, Copenhagen. Counted thread embroidery stitches worked in silk. (Courtesy National Museet, Copenhagen)

had more regular schooling. But slowly the custom spread to the country, where the designs were given a creative Scandinavian touch.

About the same time, in Amager, Denmark, cross-stitch took a unique form. King Christian II had imported Dutch farmers to teach the Danes in Amager (near Copenhagen) to grow vegetables. Out of this melting of Dutch and Danish came Amager embroidery: cross-stitch designs of animals and beings of strange, fantastical style. The area around the figures is covered with geometric shapes that fill the entire cloth and create a surprising feeling of balance. They were sewn in black silk on fine white linen because black symbolized happiness for the Amager folk. A sense of fairy tale and legend is all about these works.

Long-armed cross-stitch appeared in Scandinavian textiles at about the same time as cross-stitch and enjoyed a broader popularity in some areas. This is not surprising, for it is a stitch that progresses quickly and with an especially soothing rhythm that results in a richly textured

Detail of a corner of a handkerchief worked in Amager embroidery. (Courtesy National Museet, Copenhagen)

Section of the wall hanging from Naantali (Nådendals) Abbey Church, early sixteenth century. Long-armed cross-stitch embroidery, wool on linen. (Courtesy National Museum of Finland, Helsinki)

embroidery. Long-armed cross-stitch was most often done in wool on an extended tabby weave cloth called *tvistur*, similar to today's penelope canvas. It is from this tabby that long-armed cross-stitch gets its names, *tvistsøm* in Norwegian and *tvistsöm* in Swedish. In Iceland, where it was used before cross-stitch, it is known as *gamli krosssaumurinn* or the old cross-stitch.

From 1600 to the mid-1800s, long-armed cross-stitch took particularly magnificent forms in Iceland. It adorns many surviving ecclesiastical cloths such as altar frontals and chasubles. It reached its zenith, however, in the old Icelandic bed coverlets. Long-armed cross-stitch fills the entire surface of these bed coverlets, most of which are six feet long by five feet wide. They must have taken two or three years to make and were probably the crowning achievement of the embroiderer. The patterns look much like picture weavings of the same era; by then there were printed pattern books and even some manuscript books colored by hand that were used interchangeably for weaving, counted thread embroidery, and knitting. Doubtless, too, some

long-armed cross-stitch may have been inspired by weavings, since popular themes for both were Bible stories, animals, and legends.

Perhaps the loveliest of these coverlets is the one called *Riddarateppid* or the Coverlet of Knights, from the seventeenth century. Clothed in seventeenth-century dress, there are knights on horseback and at a banquet—all set in octagonals. On either side they are flanked by forests of deer. An intricate triple border frames the design, which is done in wools dyed deep red, blue, and green, and pale yellow and white.

What exactly the Coverlet of Knights illustrates is not known, but surely it tells a story. In folklore the stag and the hunt often have magical significance and lead people in and out of adventures. Perhaps this coverlet illustrates a folktale or heroic saga. The Icelanders, who possess a special gift of storytelling and composed most of the sagas, very naturally could have translated their stories into picture textiles. Embroiderers, having few pattern books, "saw" their designs in the stories they heard by the fireside.

Meanwhile, in Norway and Sweden long-

By contrast, the upright *gobelin* stitch may have originated as straight pattern darning, which is a technique in which the needle goes over three or four threads then under one thread, always leaving the same thread exposed so that in the end there is a striped effect. The stitching is laid smooth like satin stitch. Straight pattern darning was practiced in medieval Finland and Iceland. Upright *gobelin* is similar, but it does not leave any threads of the background cloth showing. The Norwegians call it *klostersøm*, because the technique was perfected in the monasteries in that country, where needleworkers sewed ecclesiastical embroideries to support their orders. This would date the *gobelin* stitch in Norway earlier than other counted thread stitches, because the monasteries were Catholic and mostly pre-Reformation. Little *gobelin* or double cross-stitch work has survived the centuries. Perhaps it was never as common as cross-stitch or long-armed cross-stitch.

Seventeenth-century Icelandic Coverlet of Knights bed coverlet. Wool on tvistur *worked in long-armed cross-stitch. (National Museum of Iceland, Reykjavik. Gisli Gestsson, photographer.)*

armed cross-stitch was popular for making chair and carriage or sleigh cushions. Most of these had geometric patterns of lozenges, crosses, Celtic knots, eight-petal roses, and eight-point stars. The heavy wool tapestrylike results of long-arm cross-stitch on tabby make it a very strong and durable embroidery, ideal for cushions and other well-used items.

The double cross-stitch probably developed sometime later than cross-stitch or long-armed cross-stitch. Norwegian embroiderers liked it for its rich texture and used it for geometric designs, especially variations of the eight-point star. Double cross-stitch is often known as *smyrna* in Denmark and Sweden, and diamond stitch (*diamondsting*) in Norway, because of its shape.

Härjedalen cushion embroidered in long-armed cross-stitch. The eight-point star motif is worked in red, blue, yellow, white, and dark brown wools. Note how some of the embroidery runs horizontally, while part of it runs vertically. (Courtesy Nordiska Museet, Stockholm)

The Making of the Materials

Soon after the debut of counted thread embroidery in Scandinavia came one of the most important events in the history of the textile arts: the invention of the spinning wheel, which came into common use about 1600. Until that time thread was spun with spindle and distaff—a slow process, but one the *saeter* maids considered "fine gossip work" for their long summer days tending cattle in the high mountain pastures of Norway and Sweden. The spinning wheel produced thread faster and in greater quantities and provided more supplies for weavers and embroiderers.

Making threads, yarns, and cloth were family and neighborhood efforts. From the tending of sheep and fields until finished work was worn and used, every member of the family had a hand in the process. Imagine how the cloth itself must have been full of memories and meaning.

Wool was the main material everywhere, especially in the colder climates farther north and in Iceland where flax could not be grown for linen. Almost all farms kept sheep, often tended by the older children. Finnish girls embroidered their aprons or trousseau towels while shepherding. Each spring the sheep were sheared and the oily, smelly wool was washed several times, leaving just enough lanolin to make it smooth for easy working. Then the fibers were straightened and organized by carding and spun into tough, durable, naturally water-resistant yarn. It came in a variety of colors; the first Scandinavian sheep were a dark-wooled breed, but white sheep had been imported from England in the Middle Ages. The two crossbred to produce wool in black, gray, brown, yellow, and white.

Preparing linen was less messy than working with smelly wool, and it was more of a social event. If the flax planted in spring had a good growing season, it was harvested in the late summer. Neighbors in a district went from farm to farm, helping each other pull the flax up by the roots to get the longest fibers possible, tying it into bundles, and hanging it to dry. In Sweden, the hosts

traditionally passed around a syrupy beer— *flojtedricka*— to soothe the parched, dusty throats of the harvesters. The evenings after the flax gatherings were full of merriment and song. Nothing more was done with the flax until the next summer, when it was taken down and retted in a stream to rot the remaining husks and then spread to dry on a sunny hill. The dry flax was then scraped between two wooden blades to remove the rotten husks, combed over spiked boards to straighten the fibers, and spun into thread.

Weaving often took place outside the main living hall of the farms, usually in storage buildings, where bulky looms could be set up permanently. In Sweden, Norway, and parts of Finland this was the loft house, where goods and valuables were stored, and where the farm girls slept in the warm summertime. Embroidery, being extremely portable, was done almost anywhere, and often when friends gathered together to chat. A Finnish friend, now in her seventies, remembers her grandmother knitting while herding the cattle to summer pasture or while walking over to visit neighbors; she simply tucked her yarn under her arm and knit in rhythm as she walked.

Wool and linen were dyed for counted thread embroidery, and by the seventeenth and eighteenth centuries dyeing fabrics with plant and vegetable matter was a highly developed process. Lichens were collected in late summer when their acid content was high and their colors strong and clear. Those that grew on stones were preferred to tree lichens because their colors were sharper. Most lichens produced shades of yellow, green, and brown. However, in Iceland, where few plants grow and there was no native dye for the important color red, lichens treated with urine from pregnant cows produced a bluish red. Barks were collected in late winter when the sap was in the trees. The inner layer was used fresh, or it was dried for use at a later time. Fresh bark gave the most intense colors: apple produced yellow to dark tan; birch, gray; and maple a rosy tan. Heather, taken just before it started to bloom, yielded yellow and bronze-browns. The wood, bark, and berries of juniper produced brown dyes. Mosses were gathered for dark brown colors. Mud from bogs dyed fabrics black. Woad and madder were still used for blues and reds.

By the sixteenth century dyestuffs were also being imported. Cochineal, a dried insect with a brilliant red body fluid, made rose-pink to scarlet-red dyes. Indigo, one of the oldest dyestuffs in the world, was imported from India and Egypt. A legume plant that yields a deep violet blue, indigo had to be dissolved in fermented urine before the fabric or yarn was dipped in it. Urine was often used to mordant, that is, to help fix the colors in the fibers so they did not bleed out later. Imported dyes were bought as packages of powder that was dissolved and boiled when needed.

Many villages in Scandinavia, and especially in Denmark, had a dyer's house. When farmers came to town they might bring a piece of cloth to be custom-dyed or perhaps printed, for no home dyeing could achieve the quality of reds and blues that the dyer could, nor did farmers know all the techniques for block-printing, tie-dyeing, or batik. Indeed, the dyer was considered somewhat of a magician, with his steaming pots, knowledge of chemistry, and ability to capture a sunset's red, a midnight sky's blue, or a field of flowers on cloth.

The Evolution of Home Furnishings

By this time home furnishing in peasant Scandinavia and ways of using textiles had gone through many changes. Early peoples had no tables; they reclined or squatted to eat. The first "tables" were boards laid across the laps of several banqueters at a time. Tables as we know them, and thus tablecloths, did not come to Scandinavia until the Middle Ages. At first napkins were one long ribbon of material shared by all the people on one side of the table. Personal napkins became popular in the late sixteenth century, and place mats followed in the seventeenth century. Chairs and benches came to peasant homes with the table

and were soon decorated and softened with embroidered and woven cushions. Throw pillows are a relatively recent invention. They appeared with the first upholstered furniture in the nineteenth century.

Early Scandinavian farmhouses had flueless central fireplaces or long fires, which filled the upper half of the room with smoky haze and blackened the walls with soot. No permanent decorations were possible in such an environment, so what in Old Norse is called *tjaldr* or "tent decorations" became popular for festive occasions. *Tjaldr* were light-colored fabrics that covered the entire room from the ceiling to the benches and transformed the dark rooms into a festive atmosphere, as in the Christmas Eve scene. For momentous family occasions, such as weddings and funerals, hangings were even borrowed from relatives and neighbors. The custom became so popular that it persisted into the late nineteenth century in many peasant homes, long after corner chimneys had resolved the problems of smoke and soot. The tradition lives on today in the Scandinavian fondness for wall hangings done in all kinds of embroidery and weaving techniques.

District Art

By the time of the Christmas Eve scene of 1800, some families had been settled for hundreds of years in one area, even on the same farm. In parts of Scandinavia, especially in Denmark, there was quite a bit of contact within the country and with the continent. But most of the rest of Scandinavia's peasant families were isolated on sea-hugged islands, in remote valleys separated by craggy, glacier-cloaked mountains, or between lakes and forests. Over the years the folk arts in these districts grew into specialties. Embroidery, including counted thread, was practiced everywhere, but there were regional styles, techniques, designs, and color schemes.

Cross-stitch tended to become a real specialty wherever flax grew well. Amager, Denmark, the

The Christmas table and wall and ceiling dress in the stuga *or house of the Kyrkhult farmstead from Blekinge, Sweden. (Skansen Open Air Museum, Stockholm)*

valleys of southern Norway, and central and southern Sweden in the provinces of Skåne, Blekinge, and Hälsingland (which bears as its county symbol the blue flax flower) thus became great centers of cross-stitch work and design.

Sweden especially carried on a love affair with cross-stitch in the eighteenth and nineteenth centuries. When women gathered together to socialize with their neighbors they liked to stitch, and they often shared patterns and color schemes just as they might a recipe for a delicious dish.

These people seldom traveled beyond their own parish. Over time ideas were shared enough within one parish that it came to have a characteristic cross-stitch identifiable by motif and color. The women of Blekinge favored hearts, flowers, and birds in muted tones of rose, blue, and yellow. In Skåne, tulips and acorns decorated sheets, pillowcases, and towels in somewhat brighter colors. Dalarna cross-stitch was typified by all black stitching in cotton or linen thread on a white background cloth.

A sample of Delsbo cross-stitching from the nineteenth century. Shelf border of red cotton on white cotton tabby. (Courtesy Nordiska Museet, Stockholm)

In Hälsingland there were two nearby parishes that became famous for their cross-stitch, Delsbo and Järvsö. In Delsbo parish the cross-stitchers preferred blue and red thread while in Järvsö the favorite color for cross-stitch was rose. Both parishes, however, excelled in designs of hearts and eight-point stars. They added little leaves, dangles, and crowns to the hearts, while the stars grew and branched out, metamorphosing at times into lovely snowflakes and flowers. Sometimes these lacy motifs were fitted together in an intricate design or made into borders by zigzagging lines between them. Some women got so familiar with the properties and possibilities of these motifs that

they could embellish on them as they stitched, without using a pattern. It was one of these nineteenth century Hälsingland works, a bedstead hanging embroidered in red cross-stitch on white linen that first caught my eye many years ago and prompted me to learn more about Scandinavian cross-stitch. Eventually, it inspired The Snowflake Collection in this book.

Each district in Norway, Sweden, Denmark, and Finland also developed its own distinctive costume, which was often decorated with embroidery—sometimes special regional counted thread embroidery. Counted thread embroidery was used primarily on scarves worn over the head

The hem of an apron from Äyräpää county, Finland. Multi-colored cross-stitch. (Courtesy National Museum of Finland, Helsinki)

or around the shoulders; on smocks, shifts, and shirts; or on festive aprons. Knitted mittens and hats also were brightened at times with small designs of cross-stitch or long-armed cross-stitch in gay wools counted right on to the knitting. Sometimes monograms and dates were cross-stitched in red on the white linen shirts, just under the neck slit.

Off in their corner of the world, Icelanders evolved a national art around their small population and limited natural resources. Icelandic embroidery is characterized by a finite selection of muted colors, mostly earth tones, used skillfully to create rich works. The Icelandic national costumes demonstrate this with their brown and gold vine embroidery on black wool.

The Winter Influence

During the long days of their short growing season, Scandinavian peasants labored hard coaxing what crops they could from the rocky soil. There was little time for leisure or art. It was during the northern winter, the long, dark, bitter-cold days of twilight, that folk arts thrived. Wind, snow, and ice drove people inside, where they gathered by the fire to escape the chill. Each member of the family had his or her crafts, and the long winters provided the chance to add a creative touch to each. There was no need to hurry as in the summertime.

Winter provided not only the time to create lovely and lively things, it also provided the impetus. Handcrafts added spots of cheerfulness and color that helped brighten the days—as if some bit of Scandinavian summer past had survived to remind the peasants that winter was not forever. The year would turn, and warmth and light return, but in the meantime they could bring inside the blue of their lakes, the yellow of wildflowers, the red of the midnight sun, and the other pleasures of the Scandinavian summers.

Traditions of the Home and Family

The wintertime tasks of children were to become skilled at their handcrafts. Girls and often boys learned the textile arts; they were brought up spinning, knitting, weaving, and embroidering. Over the years, a girl might begin to fill a bridal chest with her work. Someday this would become the linens for her own home. Mother, aunts, and sisters often contributed their handiwork to the cause on birthdays, name days, Christmases, and as wedding gifts, for it was a source of family pride for a young bride to have all the proper linens in her new home. In *The Decorative Arts of Sweden,* Iona Plath lists what young Swedish girls were expected to have in their bridal chests in the nineteenth century:

> Several woven woolen coverlets
> Embroidered and appliqued cushions
> Seat covers for all the chairs
> Woven runners for the benches along the
> walls
> Yards of fringed borders for the shelves and
> beams
> Wall hangings to be hung at Christmas
> Sheets, pillow cases and towels with matched
> embroidery
> Linen tablecloths with braided fringe
> An especially fine carriage cushion.

In the Finnish district of Karelia, a girl's trousseau contained several embroidered matron

hats for herself and many embroidered towels for decoration and for guests to use, for once married she was expected to keep her hair covered and be a model hostess, and she would have little time for embroidery with her new responsibilities.

For their bridal chests, girls in many parts of Scandinavia sewed large, billowy one-size-fits-all shirts that boasted their best embroidery efforts on collar, cuffs, and front placket. When they became betrothed, the girls gave these to their fiancés as wedding shirts. The significance of such a gift is recorded in the old Danish ballad, "The Long Ballad of Marsk Stig."

> Here you sit, fair lady Ingeborg;
> if you will be loyal to me,
> then sew for me a shirt
> with gold embroidery.

Similarly, young men in some districts of Norway and Sweden proposed to the girl of their choice by offering her a hand-carved *mangletraer,* a board used for ironing linens. If she accepted his gift, she was saying she would marry him. Finnish bridegrooms carved distaffs for the spinning of threads as gifts to their brides. The textile arts and the tools of the textile arts were an integral part of the traditions so important to the home and the family in Scandinavia.

For their own wedding apparel, country girls usually wore their very best district or regional

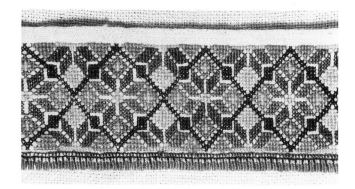

Section of cross-stitched band on a shirt from Telemark, Norway. Multi-colored wools on hemp in an eight-point star design. (Courtesy Norsk Folkemuseum, Oslo)

Two mangletraer *or mangling boards from Norway, dated 1760 and 1715, respectively. (Courtesy Norsk Folkemuseum, Oslo)*

dress, the many pieces of which they had sewn and embroidered over the years. Often there was a special headdress or bridal crown for the ceremony. Sometimes weavings or embroideries were made to commemorate the weddings. They depicted the bridal procession to the church, the traditional chain dance afterward, or the bride and groom with their initials and the date.

Textiles were a part of the other important events of life as well. One of the first things a new bride did was sew funeral clothes for herself and her husband, because peasant life was tenuous at best. For one thing, a woman stood a good chance of dying in childbirth. It would be a disgrace to her family if they did not have the proper burial clothes for her: a hand-sewn somber-hued dress that was time consuming to make. Mourners wore special clothes in black or white, depending on the customs of the area.

There were also special textiles to have ready for the coffin. Funeral blankets covered the biers on the journey from home to church. Made in subdued tones, these often had long verses or hymns stitched on them as well as symbols of

faith, such as the cross. Wide embroidered straps were used to carry the coffin and lower it into the grave. All of these funeral textiles took time to complete, and having them ready when needed was an outward sign of a woman's ability to care for her family.

When new babies were born, there was great cause for rejoicing. Baptisms were celebrated by embroidering christening gowns. In some regions special coverlets were made to bundle the baby in for the trip to the church.

Holidays and feast days offered that rare chance for the peasant peoples to take time off from their labors and gather with friends and family. Everyone wore his or her best clothes, and homes were just as richly arrayed in the finest wall and ceiling dress. Dirt or wooden floors were strewn with fresh fir clippings or sweet-smelling straw, and food was prepared weeks in advance. Tablecloths, guest towels, bed linens, and cushions completed the festive preparations. Each Scandinavian region had its own special version of these house dressings, and embroidery always played a part in them.

Distaffs made for the spinning of linen, from Vihanti, Björuö and Laihia parishes, late eighteenth and early nineteenth centuries. (Courtesy National Museum of Finland, Helsinki)

Remnant of a seventeenth-century horizontal wedding double weave from Kyrkjebø, Norway. Notice the bride with her crown in the lower left corner. (Courtesy Norsk Folkemuseum, Oslo)

This embroidery, so important in setting a mood, took a long time to complete and was highly treasured and made to last for generations. If a hole was eventually worn, it was painstakingly repaired with a matching piece of cloth on which the design was carefully reworked in exact detail. When special family linen finally wore out, Scandinavian women copied the pattern onto new cloth to use and pass on to their children just as Aunt Sigrid did; in this way a single design was used by a family for many lifetimes.

Such care was not limited to embroidery. Scandinavians seemed to be aware of future generations when making anything. Consider, for example, a farm building: the first year the farmer barked the trees to draw the resin all through the wood; the second year he felled them to cure; the third year he built with them. Such foresight paid, for many of these buildings still stand as hard and sound as rock, after hundreds of years of northern winters. In this way Scandinavian peasants did

what they could for their heirs, proud to leave a legacy of craftsmanship and beauty.

Like the farm buildings, large embroideries regularly took years to complete, but the goal was to enjoy the making as much as the results, as well as to make the results to last for generations. Such a strong sense of the continuity of time—past, present, and future—was embodied in their work. In old Scandinavia the handcrafts were a part of life and death, a means of celebrating festivities and the cycles of the year, an outward sign of love, and a part of one's cultural identity.

The peasants of Scandinavia had very little material wealth. Among their most precious possessions were the pieces of handcraft they had, in which was invested their time and creativity, or that of their friends, family, and ancestors. Counted thread embroidery was very much a part of this folk art tradition. With its simple beauty and durability, it reflects something of the common folk themselves.

Chapter Three

Folklore and Counted Thread: A Magical Kinship

As the boy raised his head, he happened to look in the glass; and then he saw that the cover to his mother's chest had been opened.

...Here she treasured all the things she had inherited from her mother, and of these she was especially careful....

While he sat there and waited for the thief to make his appearance, he began to wonder what that dark shadow was which fell across the edge of the chest. He looked and looked—and did not want to believe his eyes...It was no less a thing than an elf who sat there—astride the edge of the chest!...He had taken from the chest an embroidered piece, and sat and looked at the old-fashioned handiwork with such an air of veneration, that he did not observe the boy had awakened.

The Wonderful Adventures of Nils
Sweden, 1906, Selma Lagerlöf

The elf looking upon an old piece of embroidery with a feeling of veneration—deep respect and reverence—seems to have a special kinship with the embroidery. As he sits atop the chest he is lost in a silent communion with it. What the elf and the embroidery share is a language of symbols, a language that connects them and, in a broader sense, connects folk art and folklore. It is this language of symbols that gives the old folk art and folklore meaning for each new generation; their images have the power to convey universal truths through time.

The elf himself is a symbol coming from a symbolic world—a world that exists inside each of us, manifested in our dreams, our visions, our art, our hopes and fears. This symbolic world is shared by all peoples, and at the same time it is a deeply personal world that we each experience in our own unique way. Symbols are the shorthand for this universal yet personal inner world, and when skillfully formed into stories, they reveal the fundamental truths of the universe, of human nature, and of good and evil. Nothing speaks this symbolic language more potently or more eloquently than fairy and folktales: folklore.

The potency of folklore comes from the stripping away of detail and embellishment. Most folktales do not even name their protagonist; we have instead the youngest daughter, the widow's son, the prince or princess. There is only one time— once upon a time—which is a long ago that we can enter into again and again. Because of this the bare bones of a story are laid out for us to gnaw on: deeds and misdeeds, cowardice and courage, doubt and trust, selfishness and self-sacrificing love. And there too is the eloquence, for the folktale and the fairy tale are about each of us.

For this reason folklore has become increasingly appealing to me as a source of design for counted thread embroidery. The simplicity of detail in folklore works well with counted thread, and the power of the story imbues the design with all manner of meaning, depending on the eyes that behold it.

Counted thread, like oral tradition, is a natural medium for telling stories, for transmitting and preserving tradition, culture, history, and meaning. It is one of many visual forms of storytelling that are collectively termed "folk art." Through the language of visual symbols, counted thread can draw us in with the same sense of timelessness as does folklore. When folklore and counted thread are combined they reinforce a message, like the words "I love you" and an embrace given at the same time.

A folktale or fairy tale has several truths to tell. The meditative act of stitching, with its quietness and rhythm, can help carry us into the story so that we can explore there. As I stitch a story, I contemplate it; I become an active part of it and it a part of me.

Symbols in Scandinavian Counted Thread

Scandinavian symbols have always spoken insistently to me. This is partially because of my Scandinavian heritage: the north speaks my dialect of symbolic language.

The heart is a good example of such a Scandinavian symbol. It speaks of the need for balance between intellect, corporality, and spirituality. When these three come together in the heart, the result is love and family. Intellect or spirituality alone cannot create love or family, and sexuality alone cannot sustain them: there must be a balance as symbolized by the heart.

The eight-point star is another symbol. As a star it is a light shining in the darkness, a symbol of the spirit. But stars come in many shapes, and the number of points is relevant to the meaning. The eight-point star is four sets of points, each set of two indicating one of the cardinal directions like a compass. It is a quaternity, a symbol of wholeness.

Other cultures have symbols with these same meanings, but I do not know their dialect as well. Some symbols are universal; for instance, the roundness of an unbroken circle conveys wholeness. It may be embodied in the image of a sun, a ring, or a round stone. But the symbol also has a personal meaning for each of us, rooted in our own experiences and orientation in life. The essential truth of this symbol can be a universal message (we all seek wholeness), an intimately personal one (we each have a different route to take to reach that wholeness), and a cultural one (the route for one culture may be different from that of another).

Symbols seem fairly constant and unalterable, yet that is not quite so. Nuances come and go and occasionally, a cataclysmic event occurs to alter one profoundly, as happened to the swastika, which is an ancient Scandinavian textile symbol (see Överhogdal photograph, p. 17). The swastika is found in almost every ancient culture in the Old and New World. It represents variously the supreme deity, the sun, or the points of the compass, which are all related to quaternity or the numina—the mystic center. The word itself is Sanskrit for "well-being" or "benediction," which was why Kipling used it to decorate his books. But Hitler's use of it as his Nazi party emblem and symbol of anti-Semitism inverted it and perverted it, so that what it communicates now is negative and horrifying. Hitler's awareness of the symbol was only superficial; to the deeper meanings of it he was impervious.

Symbols in Scandinavian Folklore

The symbols in Scandinavian folklore also call to me. The vivid images appeal to a hunger for romanticism and enchantment, and at the same time give me glimpses into my own nature, light and dark. Scandinavian folklore satisfies my desire for both the real and the magical, and the images it communicates quite naturally translate into design ideas—indeed sometimes I am flooded by the images Scandinavian folklore can generate, for it grew in rich soil.

In Scandinavia, folklore was unimpeded by the different trends of rationalism and other forces working in more cosmopolitan areas. These forces sought to deny the symbolism of folklore and the mysticism of faith and worked only with realism. Among isolated Scandinavian peasants symbolic language flowered. That is why Scandinavian folk art is not concerned with realism; the lack of perspective, shading, and proportions is intentional. Scandinavian embroiderers and other highly skilled folk artists were simply not as interested in realism as in what their figures and designs represented. Their instincts told them that symbols are most powerful when they are simple, just as they are in folklore.

But the power of symbols in folklore and folk art, the power to evoke an awakening, to touch something inside us, is a potency that is sometimes lost when these symbols are used today. Elves and their kin have dwindled and heroes and heroines become inflated and empty. Thus muddled, they are unable to speak as they once did.

THE HERO

Early Scandinavians had a particularly deep respect for and appreciation of heroes. In old Norse mythology there was no eternal life; one's only chance for immortality was through accomplishing heroic deeds, which, if they were great enough, would be celebrated in verse long after death. So it was for Sigurth and Beowulf.

We live in an age of shallow heroes, and it hurts us. Children especially need thoughtful heroes to emulate, such as those in folklore. From them children learn how to face the struggles and weaknesses in their own lives, and from their mistakes children learn many invaluable lessons about battling their own dragons and monsters. They learn integrity and courage and generosity, without which life becomes mundane at best, and viscious, bitter, and selfish at worst.

When I was growing up, I had some real-life folk heroes. They were my Latvian friend's parents—World War II refugees forced out of their homeland when they would not conform to the ways of those who took power. They walked hundreds of miles across Europe with their young child and a small cart of possessions seeking a new life. They are common people who at a crucial point in their lives showed extraordinary courage and principle. They gave me hope that if I ever had to, I might be able to do the same.

The loss of heroes is reflected in modern needlework design, first of all by the conspicuous absence of folklore as a design source. But also in designs that caricature Vikings as savages or silly cartoon figures, much like American Indians used to be pictured. Yet the great hero Beowulf was a Viking, and Vikings were explorers of new worlds. Needlework that belittles such folk heroes has lost touch with the language of symbols. Such bankrupt images will not speak over time.

For the hero is finally an example for us, a model of how life should be lived. A hero can be a common man or woman with weaknesses and flaws, yet with a virtue that enables him or her to acknowledge mistakes and with the courage to seek truth and good.

THE IMAGINARY BEING

Just as the hero is one facet of our humanness, our own heroic side, so the elf and all imaginary beings represent, among other things, yet another part of us—our shadow, the hidden corners of our soul. (Does the boy not first perceive the elf as a shadow?) It is no coincidence that the myth of the *huldre*-folk—the Scandinavian elves or "hidden people"—explains them as the unwashed children of Eve, whom she hid away from God in shame when he asked to see her offspring.

Yet in post-Victorian literature, art, and thought something has happened to the imaginary beings we call fairy folk: elves, fairies or *huldre*-folk, trolls, *nisser* (Swedish *tomtem*, Finnish *haltiga*), or dwarves. In their original form these symbolic creatures were formidable, dangerous, and often deadly. People feared them, just as the characters do in Sigrid Undset's *Kristin Lavransdatter*, a novel set in medieval Norway. "She knew that in the wild woods wolves and bears lorded it, and that under every stone there dwelt trolls and goblins and elfin-folk, and she was afraid..."

But with the twentieth century, whimsy came into literature and took all of the danger and mystery out of fairy folk. It made them diminutive harmless, and uninspiring: a "painty-winged, wand-waving, sugar-and-shake-your-head set of imposters" as Rudyard Kipling put it in his story "Cold Iron." It is not simply that we do not believe in fairy folk anymore, it is that we do not want to acknowledge our own dark side. This dark side is not easily denied, however, and it has taken new symbolic form in alien beings from outer space and a whole new genre of monsters, most only plastic imitations of the meaty imaginary beings from folklore.

This whimsy has crept into folk art, too, including needlework. The *nisser*—not the *Julenisse,* who has become a type of Santa Claus, but the temperamental hobgoblin guardian spirits of the old Scandinavian farms—have been demoted to sugary sweet cereal box images. In modern embroidery design the word *nisser* has actually come to be a synonym for images of impish but very human and benign children more than any kind of hobgoblin.

Trolls, too, have dwindled to much less than they originally were. Now they have mushroom hats, sweet grins, and only one head. About all that is left of their former huge, stonelike, multi-headed selves is a long nose. Yet folklore tells us that at one time trolls lurked in the dark forests and wild mountains of the north, rattling the world with their periodic outbursts and eating human flesh when they could get it. From the body of their ancestor, the frost giant, Ymir, the earth was formed. In the end, at Ragnarok, it will be these monsters against the heroes and the gods (and the heroes and gods are destined to lose). But now even trolls have become harmless.

Diluted images of fairy folk are not satisfying. They tell us nothing about our world and ourselves. We not only long for them to breathe somewhere in the visible distance, but to have power both good and evil. If not, then our sojourns in their land can never be heroic. J. R. R. Tolkien,

the great fantasy writer, says of the fairy folk world we hunger for:

> The realm of fairy-story is wide and deep and high and filled with many things: all manner of beasts and birds are found there; shoreless seas and stars uncounted; beauty that is an enchantment and an ever-present peril; both joy and sorrow as sharp as swords…. ("On Fairy Stories," *The Tolkien Reader*)[4]

Both joy and sorrow as sharp as swords: it is the sorrow that makes the joy precious. The enchanting beauty is heightened by the sense of peril. In the old Scandinavian textiles, as in folklore, the joy and sorrow and the enchantment intrigue us still. "…they open a door on Other Time, and if we pass through, though only for a moment, we stand outside our own time, outside Time itself, maybe." (Tolkien)

The Door to Time

I want my counted thread embroidery designs to capture the enchantment and the joy and the sorrow. I want to use symbols with a respect and understanding that will allow them their full power. I would like to open that door on other time and experience just a fraction of the timelessness that is in the Skog and Överhogdal hangings, the Öseberg and Bayeux tapestries.

But is all this really necessary for embroidery projects today? Perhaps not. Yet understanding of the language of symbols can deepen the enjoyment of embroidery. Frivolity and whimsy are not bad, but they tend to be limited in time; they have a short life. If you are stitching not only for yourself and today but for the future, a sensitivity to symbols will help your work to go beyond fad and fashion toward timelessness. After all, some pieces of needlework take months and even years to complete. What could be worse than having them lose their appeal because they go out of fashion before they are even finished? In order to be a medium for transmitting and preserving tradition and meaning, counted thread must be in touch with the language of symbols; otherwise, it is simply a picture whose meaning fades over time.

The elf in Lagerlöf's story recognizes the timelessness in the old embroidery he venerates. On the other hand Nils, the young protagonist of the story, venerates nothing: not his parents, not the church, not nature nor history and art—nothing. He cares only for himself. The book tells the story of Nils' physical and spiritual journey out of this self-centeredness when he is turned into a small elf and caught by chance in the migrations of the geese. Nils, too, comes to understand the magic language of symbols, which connects us to each other and our entire world, even to a flock of wild geese.

Nils' mother is another character in the story who values the old embroidery. She treasures it because it is a family heirloom given to her by her mother. Through the old embroidery and its symbols, Nils' mother is connected to her family with an immediacy that crosses the barriers of time and death. It is a connection with generations she knew and generations she never knew. Through the old embroidery she can stand outside time itself and transcend time, just like magic.

The elf saw all of this magic in the old embroidery; the same magic that is in him, the magic of symbol, of something beyond words and beyond time. Nils' mother stored her old embroidery with great care. Had they met, she and the elf would have had much to say to each other.

Chapter Four
Old in a New Way

Then the king ordered Herot cleaned
And hung with decorations: hundreds of hands,
Men and women, hurried to make
The great hall ready. Golden tapestries
Were lined along the walls, for a host
Of visitors to see and take pleasure in...

Beowulf
Burton Raffel, translator
England, eighth century

The long Scandinavian tradition of hand-crafted textiles has inspired my own counted thread designs. This tradition has an immediacy; it belongs not only to the past but also to the present and is ours to celebrate. The Danish have a saying about this: *gammelt på en ny måde*, "old in a new way."

The many Scandinavian traditions and symbols—ancient and folk—that have influenced my work are discussed in the preceding chapters. They have been not only the sources of my embroidery themes, but have made their mark on my style and artistic philosophy. As with Scandinavian textile artists before me, I am not so much interested in realism as in symbolic meaning and in the expressive power of simple motifs.

At the same time, my counted thread designs are somewhat of a divergence from tradition. For one thing, they are very much of the twentieth century. And they are not purely Scandinavian, but Scandinavian-American.

There are several other ways in which my "old in a new way" is new. The most obvious to me is in the materials for counted thread embroidery, which are now mostly factory made. There is no denying that we have lost something in using chemically dyed materials rather than those colored with vegetable dyes. Yet we have gained a greater variety of colors, which is growing ever larger as manufacturers work to meet the demands of designers and embroiderers. We also have colors that better withstand cleaning. There is still plenty of natural material to be found: cotton, linen, and wool, of excellent quality. Twentieth-century synthetics add variety and versatility. I still prefer to use natural materials, but for household and wearable embroidery, the synthetics are very practical.

What follows are my original counted thread embroidery designs in five collections, all based on Scandinavian textile traditions and folk symbols. Each collection contains from five to twenty different embroidery designs, centered around a motif or theme. There are fifty-eight designs in all. The graphic patterns for these designs can be found in Chapter Six.

The Homestead Collection
(colorplates 1–7)

Carved bowl, circa 1700, from Bykle, Setesdal, Norway. (Courtesy Norsk Folkemuseum, Oslo)

The Homestead Collection celebrates the farms and fjords of Norway, my ancestral Scandinavian home. I have walked in the steep meadows above the fjords of Norway, among the old log farm buildings; looked down into the deep water, blue and clear, and beyond to more hills breeching like whales snout first, sheer and rocky. I have picnicked in those meadows with sheep and a sturdy little fjord pony or two, and the next morning awoke to breakfast with freshly laid eggs.

Most of the land in Norway is so rocky that it is amazing the farms have ever existed at all, let alone for hundreds of years. They dot the hillsides somewhat sparsely, obviously placed where arable soil can be found. The joke is that the grazing animals all have longer legs on one side and shorter legs on the other from centuries spent on the steep slopes.

For this collection I have created nearly twenty different pieces of needlework, many of which can be used in more than one way. All are centered around the rural peasant life of Norway.

HOMESTEAD TABLE RUNNER AND BELLPULL

Domestic animals were essential to the existence of the Norwegian farms: without the horse a peasant could not travel far; without sheep there would be no wool to warm the winters; without chickens there would be no eggs and less meat. Stylized versions of these animals commonly decorated folk art as proud symbols of Norwegian farm life. They seem to be just as prolific in my designs, covering Table Runner, Bellpull, samplers, pillows, pictures, and clothing.

The peasant couple on the Homestead Table Runner and Bellpull are not in regional costume. Rather their dress is my own fantastic rendition of a Norwegian peasant couple—perhaps as they might be in a folktale. These pieces are in the traditional Norwegian gold, orange-red, gray-blue, and brown black, which first developed out of the range of colors given by natural vegetable dyes in Scandinavia.

THE NORSEMAN SAMPLER

The peasants of Norway, men and women alike, were always free landowners, never serfs or bondsmen. Their land had great meaning to them, and they passed it on from generation to generation. The Norseman Sampler is based on a verse from "Nordmannen" by Ivar Aasen.

Millom bakker og berg ut med havet
heve nordmannen fenge sin heim,
der han sjølv heve tuftene grave
og sett sjølv sine hus uppå deim

Mong the rocks by the North Sea's blue waters
The proud Norseman his homestead has found,
There does he and his sons and daughters,
Claim inherited right to the ground.

This collection of counted thread designs is also a celebration of the folk art of Norway, which began and thrived on these farms among the *almue*, "the common people." Many buildings were carved on the outside with graceful scrolls and lines. The *stabbur* or loft house, where grain and valuables

Loft house or stabbur *and* bur *from Rofshus, Telemark, Norway. (Courtesy Norsk Folkemuseum, Oslo)*

were stored, was the most important farm building and usually had the most extensive carvings. Many of the old buildings now are in the open air museums across Norway, where they have been moved and preserved for all to enjoy. The two buildings pictured in the samplers are in the Norsk Folkemuseum in Oslo. The *stabbur* dates from 1754 from Telemark in southern Norway. The house or *barfrøstue* is from Glåmdal and was built in 1670.

Sognefjord, in western Norway, as seen from the hills above the little village of Flåm, inspired the landscape of The Norseman Sampler.

GUDBRANDSDAL DOLLS

The couple and the sheep in The Norseman Sampler found their way onto a few other needlework pieces including a set of dolls.

Norwegian peasants often embroidered their clothing, especially their best dress for church and festive occasions, since known as folk costumes. This couple wears a version of the costume from the valley of Gudbrandsdal in Norway. The embroidery is a lovely free embroidery called *roseaum* or "rose embroidery," adapted from rosemaling in the eighteenth century. The Gudbrandsdal costume, or *bunad,* nearly died out after the Industrial Revolution, but a turn-of-the-century folk revival brought renewed interest, and the *bunad* was reconstructed in the 1920s from an old skirt in the Oslo Folkemuseum.

These were the first dolls I designed, and I

enjoyed them so much and became so intrigued by folk costumes that I designed an entire collection of dolls in costumes from across Scandinavia. The Gudbrandsdal dolls are a freer rendition than those in The Folk Costume Collection. The girl does not wear an apron or a purse, which are sometimes used with the Gudbrandsdal dress. The man wears rolled-up trousers and his farm boots.

SHEEP TABLE SET

The sheep provides one of the most important materials for the making of textiles in Scandinavia. And with its folklore and Biblical significance, the sheep is rich in symbolism.

The Sheep Table Set consists of place mats, napkins, and breadcovers. The place mat motif can be continued on a longer piece of fabric for a shelf border or tablecloth border or even run down the two sides of a table runner.

HOMESTEAD PICTURES

I also borrowed the sheep, the chickens, and the Gudbrandsdal couple out from The Norseman Sampler and put them in their own designs. These can be used for pillows or baskets or simply framed as pictures for the wall.

THE BABY'S ROOM SAMPLER

Children are a farm's blessing. While I was working with the sheep motif, I began playing with the phrase "sheep sleep sweet." Out of it grew a little verse for a Baby's Room Sampler:

> Peep peep peep
> Sheep sleep sweet
> So shall you
> Tucked in neat.

Like The Norseman Sampler, The Baby's Room Sampler is richly dressed in Norwegian folk art, only here it is furniture and baby clothing. Traditionally the grandfathers-to-be made the cradles. Mothers, aunts, and grandmothers embroidered simple, roomy cloths for the babies.

BIBS AND JUMPER

From The Baby's Room Sampler I took the sheep and chick and put them on bibs. The sheep and hearts I also transferred to the yoke on a little girl's jumper.

ROSEMALING PICTURE FRAMES

Another great folk art tradition in Norway is the folk painting. The Norwegian peasants decorated their houses and their furniture and utensils with the stylized petals and curves of rosemaling or rosepainting, which developed in the eighteenth century and became very popular. Some districts such as Telemark and Hallingdal were renowned for their rosemaling, and artists from those areas traveled all over making their living by custom painting homes. From this tradition developed the needle art of *roseaum*, such as decorates the women's costume from Gudbrandsdal and other districts. These arts are echoed in the curves of the little picture frame designs, which are sized to hold snapshots.

THE LORD'S PRAYER SAMPLER

Norwegian peasants often expressed their faith through their needlework with verses, prayers, or Biblical illustrations such as Adam and Eve by the Tree of Knowledge, angels, and the crucifixion. I wanted to design a sampler for this collection using part of the Old Norse Lord's Prayer. I also wanted to try the fjord scene and farm buildings from The Norseman Sampler in very different colors, using mauves and roses instead of reds. The result is The Lord's Prayer Sampler.

> *Fader vor du some er in himlene*
> *helliget vorde dit navn.*

> Our Father Who Art in heaven
> hallowed be thy name.

For the Norwegian farmers faith went hand-in-hand with a feeling of hospitality and welcoming toward the rest of the world. In response I put *velkommen* across the top of the sampler. Welcome, friend, come in and be welcome.

The Snowflake Collection
(colorplates 7–11)

The Snowflake Collection was inspired by a nineteenth-century bedstead hanging from Hälsingland, Sweden. Hälsingland, with its crop of high-quality flax, has long been a center of first-rate Swedish cross-stitch. Among the many pieces of old Hälsingland cross-stitch that are preserved are some of the loveliest renditions of the eight-point star I have ever seen. This Hälsingland bedstead hanging, like many, is stitched in red cotton thread on bleached linen. Its design is an

experiment in geometric leaves, eight-point stars, and lacy zigzags. They were meant more to be stylized flowers, perhaps, but within the graceful geometry I saw glimpses of snowflakes.

Snowflakes are, of course, important symbols in a winter world like Scandinavia. There the snowflake is often derived from a more universal symbol, the eight-point star, which came up from Egypt, probably during the Migration Period (A.D. 200–800) and became popular throughout Europe. In some areas it remained a star, while in other regions it also became a round-petalled rose. In Scandinavia it is just as often a snowflake. (Real snowflakes are six-pointed, but the geometry of counted thread works best in eight-point figures.) No matter which of these shapes it takes, the eight-point symbol contains a sense of symmetry and wholeness. However, as a snowflake there is something temporal and fragile about it.

The eight-point star is also the basis of my snowflake designs, with the points sometimes

Hälsingland bedstead hanging, nineteenth century. Red cross-stitch on white cotton ground. (Courtesy Nordiska Museet, Stockholm)

fused and sometimes multiplied to make each snowflake slightly different. The bellpull was the first piece I designed. The same snowflakes are arranged to make the design for the table runner. From these two designs came the pictures, tree decorations, and other smaller pieces. You may find new pieces to create from these designs.

The snowflake is often combined in Scandinavian designs with another northern symbol, the reindeer. The asymmetrical reindeer makes a good contrast, while the laciness of reindeer horns echoes the snowflake spokes. This particular reindeer is taken from traditional Lapp embroidery. I like his pluckiness, and he looks quite at home among eight-point stars and snowflakes.

Bits of Christmas
(colorplates 11–16)

It seems almost as if there are as many Christmas traditions in Scandinavia as there are stars in the sky, and each one takes on different flavors as mood and fancy vary from region to region. Preparations are begun weeks in advance, for in all of the Scandinavian countries this is the big holiday of the year. The designs in this chapter are really only a small taste of the richness of Scandinavian Christmas tradition and symbolism, but as with all things rich, I hope this small quantity goes a long way.

CHRISTMAS STOCKINGS

This book really began in earnest when I designed the Christmas stocking for our son. It was not my first design, but it was where my sense of Scandinavian symbols first came together. When our daughter was born, I made a stocking for her too, again delighting in the chance to use many of the symbols that had become meaningful to me.

At the tops of these stockings are snowflakes—symbols of winter. But below them grow trees and flowers—signs of renewal and hope. The reindeer is magical; wherever it comes there is adventure and enchantment. The hearts are love and family and faith. Saint Lucia, with her headdress of candles, symbolizes the return of light after darkness, just as the year turns from the dead of winter to the longer days of spring, and the babe in the manger brings new light to the weary world.

Santa Claus, who is known by many names in Scandinavia, comes to leave children gifts, sometimes in stockings but more often under the tree. In Finland, he is the Christmas goat, *Julubukki*, the descendant of an ancient pagan symbol, jovial and boisterous. In Norway he is *Julenisse* and in Sweden *Jultomte*, loosely translated "Christmas elf" or "Christmas spirit." He carries his big bag over his shoulder and asks "are there any good children here?" His reindeer, of course, are all of Scandinavian descent.

LUCIA BRIDE TABLE RUNNER, BELLPULL, AND PICTURE

Saint Lucia is important enough in Scandinavia to merit her own day during Yule, 13 December. On that morning the youngest daughter rises early in order to prepare hot coffee and saffron buns to serve to the rest of the family. In the tradition of Saint Lucia, she wears a long white gown and on her head, a crown of lighted candles. Lucia means "light," and Saint Lucia was a young Sicilian in the early church who gave her life for her faith; a light as witness to the Light.

Lucia Bride festivals have become traditions in many places among Scandinavians and Scandinavian-Americans. They are a chance not only to crown a Lucia Bride and experience a lovely ceremony, but also to offer the first sampling of holiday music and baking, and sometimes an opportunity to enjoy folk costumes and folk dancing as well.

THE BETHLEHEM SCENE

Finally in this collection is a Bethlehem Scene. It was inspired by post-Reformation Biblical picture weavings and embroideries of Scandinavia. These textiles often illustrate the Bethlehem Scene—

Mary holding Jesus or the Three Wise Men approaching the manger with gifts. Although some are rough in design, others strike me with the tenderness and emotion they convey. As I began to work through an idea of a Madonna design, I became intrigued with the showing of emotion and expression through a few simple lines—Mary holding Jesus...the mother holding her newborn child on "night of all nights, Christmas Night." What was Mary feeling then? Surely she, more than any woman, knew the bittersweetness of motherhood. Yet she did not hesitate in her new-found maternity, but on the contrary seemed to know great peace in it all and in the moment, the overwhelming joy of the birth of a child.

In the dark winter chill the festival of Christmas brings family and friends together in love and good cheer to celebrate the magic, to celebrate the hope of renewal, to celebrate the Light.

The Folk Costume Collection
(colorplates 17–20)

Together the five Scandinavian countries can claim over eight hundred folk costumes, ranging from Iceland's handful of national dresses, to Sweden's more than four hundred regional or local costumes. Folk costumes are peasant dress. They are the best dress of the working class and are saved for festive occasions and Sundays. The middle and upper classes sometimes tried to copy folk dress in an occasional romantic urge to experience what they thought of as a carefree existence, but such attempts always had modern and upper class features.

I used to think the folk costumes of Scandinavia were ancient, perhaps as old as the countries themselves. But the fact is that their history is relatively recent. Most medieval Scandinavian peasants dressed in simple tunics and shifts of undyed wool and wadmal, as did most of the peasantry of Europe. Costume dress began as early as the sixteenth century, but fully developed regional folk dress is a phenomenon of the eighteenth and early nineteenth centuries, when there was enough prosperity to have a few luxuries such as a set of clothes reserved just for special occasions.

Once Scandinavian folk dress came about, it changed very slowly compared to fashions in the rest of Europe and even in the Scandinavian upper classes. This was due in large part to the isolation of Scandinavian peasants in each of their districts. It was also because a costume took years to sew and embroider, and most women had only one in their entire lifetime. Most of us would probably find it hard to imagine having one dress serve as wedding dress, church dress, and attire for every special occasion. The costume even had planned adjustments to accommodate pregnancy and weight change.

In some areas, dress became intimately tied to the church year calendar. Little details were changed for certain seasons, church festivals, and especially solemn Sundays. It became quite a complicated social custom. Politics also played a part; in eighteenth-century Sweden, anti-luxury ordinances forbade the use of imported materials such as silk, and levied taxes on luxury items such as wigs and hooped skirts. These made imported goods prohibitive to the peasants, who were mostly landowners but still never had much in the way of cash. So most of the costumes developed around native materials such as homespuns and country weaves. This was true everywhere but in parts of Denmark, which being more central to Europe and more involved in trade used Oriental silk in some costumes.

In some parts of Scandinavia it was frowned upon to change any details on a costume, while in others, touches of individuality were encouraged. Aprons and purses or "pockets" were sometimes required, sometimes optional. Men's dress often included a hunting knife, which was sometimes hung on a special belt. However, most areas had very strict social rules dictating different dress for unmarried girls, matrons, and people in mourning. The most universal of these rules was the covering of the head for married women.

In the mid-nineteenth century new values swept through Scandinavia, and the traditional costume went into disuse in many parts and totally disappeared in some. The Industrial Revolution, with its inexpensive factory textiles and its philosophy of "newer is better" was a part of this change. So was a conservative religious movement that spread through parts of Scandinavia, preaching simplicity in dress, forbidding bright colors, and frowning upon folk music and other folk customs as pagan.

The folk costume tradition might have been lost completely if not for a romantic revival of folk customs in Scandinavia in the decades around the turn of the twentieth century. Antiquarians and folklorists rounded up what existing costumes they could find at that time, documented them and collected them in some museums. Other costumes were reconstructed from bits and pieces that could be found or from old paintings or photographs. Regions that had either lost their folk costumes or never had any created new ones.

Today there is a strong interest in folk costumes. They are a living tradition as a part of folk dance groups and a way for people of Scandinavian descent to celebrate their heritage and their common interests. They are also important to anyone interested in folk customs or textile work in general.

But how does a needlework designer who wants to illustrate a representative folk costume or two from each Scandinavian country choose only a dozen out of nearly a thousand? It is not an easy task. I am attracted to just about every folk costume I see. For this collection I chose to illustrate costumes from areas that have strong histories of textile folk arts. It is a way to celebrate those areas and to pay homage to their great art.

All of these folk costume designs are based on research done by experts in Scandinavian folk costumes, many of whom are present or former curators of museums in Scandinavia.

DANISH COSTUMES—*FOLKEDRAGTER*

The Danish figures are dressed in costumes

"Hedebopige," *illustrating the folk dress of the time in Hedebo, Denmark, 1864, by F. C. Lund.*

from the area of Hedebo-engnen, near Copenhagen. Hedebo is famous for Hedebo embroidery, a lovely technique of open work embroidery with soft curves in white.

The woman's costume is based on *Hedebopige,* one of a series of paintings of peasants in costume by the nineteenth-century Danish artist F. C. Lund. The color combination of red, green, and white is fresh and pleasant. Her vest and skirt are of hand-woven wool. The trim at the bottom of the skirt is silk ribbon, which originally was used to hide worn hems and later became purely decorative. She wears a matron's hat and a cotton neckerchief with lace trim.

Hedebo boasts several variations of its

costumes. This man's costume is taken from *Folkedragter* by Minna Kragelund, in association with the Danish Folkemuseum. I chose this particular one not only because the color goes so nicely with the woman's costume, but because of the interesting broad-brimmed hat and exceptionally long coat. Both of the Danish figures wear the black folk costume shoes common throughout Scandinavia.

FINNISH COSTUMES—*KANSALLISPUKU*

Finland is a meeting of worlds, which makes for a striking variety of costumes. The area along the western border once belonged to Sweden, and the costumes there share similarities with those of Sweden: vertically striped skirts, white or solid-colored aprons, shawls, and lace-trimmed hats. On the eastern border of Finland next to Russia is an area called Karelia. The costumes there show a strong Baltic influence—fringed aprons boldly striped in horizontal reds and blues, headbands or headdresses, and large silver medallions.

It was very difficult to decide, but I finally chose to clothe the Finnish figures in Karelian costume. Their Baltic flavor makes a nice contrast to the other costumes in this collection, and Karelia has a strong history of cross-stitch embroidery.

Finns from Antea parish in the eastern district of Karelia in folk costume, 1860 by Magnus von Wright. (Courtesy National Museum of Finland, Helsinki)

These costumes are based on photographs from *Kansallispukuja* by Helmi Vuorelma Oy, published in Finland.

The woman's costume is from Antrea, Karelia. The bold red and white striped apron is woven, then fringed. The headdress with the big red tassels hanging down is braided or wound around a frame. It is one of several common Karelian headdresses for married women. Unmarried women wear ribbons tied across their foreheads in headbands.

The man's costume comes from Seiskari, Karelia. The blue stockings are hand knit in a special pattern. His wool pants are white and his vest has a narrow horizontal stripe of red and white. Like the woman, he wears leather moccasins rather than black folk costume shoes. At his side hangs his hunting knife.

ICELANDIC COSTUME—*UPPHLUTUR*

Iceland has three women's costumes, all national and differentiated according to their degree of formality. All are decorated with free embroidery.

The everyday costume or *upphlutur* is the one I have chosen to illustrate in counted thread embroidery. It has a black wool skirt and matching sleeveless bodice or vest, which is embroidered in a floral motif using gilt metal thread and laced together with a long chain. The apron is white or vertically striped in earth tones. There is a small tasseled cap that sits on the back of the head.

I based this design on the costume in the booklet *The National Costume of Women in Iceland* by Elsa E. Gudjónsson, curator of textiles at the National Museum of Iceland in Reykjavik.

NORWEGIAN COSTUME—*BUNADER*

The name Hardanger embroidery is well-known among embroiderers. Named for the area around the western Norwegian fjord where it originated, Hardanger work is a geometric style of satin stitching and cutwork that has a crisp, neat look to it. More than two hundred years ago the

Norwegian women from Stavanger wearing folk dress similar to Hardanger costumes, 1905. There are differences between the costumes, especially in the embroidery of the apron, but the Stavanger costumes are obviously greatly influenced by the ones from Hardanger. (Author's private collection)

women's costume of Hardanger was developed around this embroidery. During the romantic revival of folk ways, this costume became very popular all over Norway. An old family picture from around 1905 shows my great great great aunts from Stavanger—quite a ways south of Hardanger Fjord—in costumes very much like the modern Hardanger dress.

Perhaps the most striking part of this costume is the Hardanger embroidered apron of open geometric cutwork set against a dark blue or black wool skirt. The tucker in the red vest and the belt are embroidered in beadwork. The eight-point star is often used as a motif for the costume's embroidery. Young girls wear embroidered headbands, brides are decked in an ornate silver-gilt crown, and matrons wear stiff starched white kerchiefs or coifs to cover their hair, a holdover from medieval traditions.

The man's Hardanger costume dates from the early 1800s. It has a short jacket sporting a straight high collar, trousers or knickers all in black wool, and knitted white stockings. Red, yellow, and green stitching accent the outfit. The costumes for these figures are based on folk dress in Kjirsti Skavhaug's *Norwegian Bunads.*

SWEDISH COSTUMES—*FOLKDRÄKTER*

Because Sweden has over four hundred folk costumes—nearly half of all the Scandinavian costumes—I decided to design three Swedish figures: a couple from Hälsingland and a little girl in Dalarna dress.

The Hälsingland district of Sweden, famous for its flax and counted thread embroidery, also has a very old and rich costume history. This man's costume was exhibited at Nordiska Museet in Stockholm as early as 1875. It has a short jacket and knickers in a traditional dark blue. Leather boots and an old-style red and blue broadcloth hat complete the outfit. It represents the Bjuraker parish in Hälsingland.

The woman's costume is also from Bjuraker. It boasts a lot of red and dark blue, the Scandinavian colors of prosperity. The red bodice, dark blue skirt with broad red band, and blue and white striped apron are all of wool. The multicolored shawl is of imported silk and varies somewhat for each individual costume. This woman wears an embroidered matron's hat. The Hälsingland costumes are based on the drawings in Anna-Maija Nylen's *Folkdräkter,* published by Nordiska Museet in 1949 when Nylen was curator there.

The third Swedish costume is from the district of Dalarna. This little girl wears the costume of

Sundborn parish, which was the home of the great Swedish painter Carl Larsson and his textile-artist wife, Karin. Sundborn had no costume tradition, so in 1902 this one was composed with the help of the Larssons. Carl Larsson, who loved to paint his home and family, often posed his daughters in costume, and this figure is taken from one of those paintings, *Karin at the Window,* a print of which hangs in my daughter's room. The dress is a sunny yellow, the apron a bold orange and black vertical stripe. A rose-patterned shawl and child's bonnet round out the festive dress.

LAPP COSTUME—*BUNADER*

The Lapps of Scandinavia are a separate and distinctive group of people, living in family tribes in the extreme north. Most are seminomadic, following the reindeer herds across parts of Norway, Sweden, Finland, and Siberia, although some are settled on the coast as fishermen and hunters. The Lapps have unique costumes, which up until recent years they wore for everyday as well as special occasions. The costumes vary from family to family and area to area in shade of blue, trim pattern, and hat shape, but most are the same basic style of full tunic for both men and women. The men wear theirs shorter with reindeer skin pants underneath.

These figures are dressed in the Lapp costumes of Finmark, Norway. The blue of the costume is very bright, and the trim is a riot of red, yellow, green, and white. The full tunics can be worn alone in warmer weather or over many layers of sweaters in winter. The woman's hat is bright red, with cheek guards that can be tied close around the face as protection from the biting wind. Lapp women wear dark blue stockings and reindeer skin shoes, which are ideal for walking in snow. The colorful wrappings around the ankles hold the tops of the shoes closed to keep the snow out. The Lapp boy wears reindeer skin pants and boots. His high Lapp hat has the same trim on it as is on his tunic, and a flowing blue scarf is tied around it. The costumes for these figures are from *Vare vaker bunader* by Yngve Woxholth.

The Folklore Collection
(colorplates 20-24)

Scandinavia has a literary heritage uncommonly rich in myth, legend, folktales, and fairy tales. Many of the images and symbols are familiar folklore motifs found around the world, but here they have a certain feel that marks them indelibly as Scandinavian. And, as with folk costumes, they are not only identifiable as Scandinavian as a whole, but as one comes to know their subtler nuances, it is possible to identify characteristics that make them particularly of one country or another: the romanticism of the Danes, the straightforward pragmatism of the Finns, the poetic drama of the Icelanders, the earthiness of the Swedes, the Norwegian flight of fancy, the primitive magic of the Lapps. After their centuries of struggling for survival in their harsh, cold climate, all have a deep awareness of the elemental forces of the universe and the precariousness of life in such a world. Their literary traditions are woven with strong threads of introspection and melancholy, yet not despair, and all are embroidered with a resilient sense of humor that allows them to laugh even at their own fate.[5]

The folktales of these countries—the magical beasts, folk heroes, wry humor, and enchantment—are every bit as fascinating and relevant today as when told by skalds a thousand years ago or by peasants warming themselves around the fire on Scandinavian homesteads.

Out of the vast, brimming pool of Scandinavian folklore I have hooked one morsel from each country to illustrate in counted thread embroidery. There is an heroic legend from Iceland, folktales from Finland and Norway, fairy tales from Denmark and Sweden, and from Lapland a magic symbol.

THE SNOW QUEEN—DENMARK

In the spring of 1805 a little boy was born into the poverty of a Danish cobbler's house. He was deeply loved by his parents, and his father made him puppets and toys in his spare time. But his father died when the boy was young, so at fourteen Hans Christian Andersen, who had always been a sensitive child and a dreamer, went to Copenhagen to try his fortune as an actor and writer.

At acting he was not particularly successful. He tried writing novels, poetry, plays, and ballads, but for years these were also unsuccessful. Then finally in 1835, when he was thirty years old, one of his novels gained popularity. That same year Andersen published a small pamphlet containing four original fairy tales, including "The Princess and the Pea." They were considered amusing and charming and a great success. Andersen had found his element, and he settled into writing fairy tales. As he wrote, people began to realize that "he was doing something entirely new in literature: combining the traditional form and colloquial flavor of the folktale with the insights of an original and highly individual mind."[6]

Andersen continued to write fairytales and became beloved by his fellow Danes in his own lifetime. He read his stories to children and kings alike. In the opening to his autobiography he says, "My life is a wonderful fairy tale."

"The Snow Queen" is one of Andersen's best works. It is the story of Kay and Gerda, poor but very happy children, and best friends. Their families live in adjacent attics, and Kay and Gerda converse from close-set windows over little flower boxes. Then one day Kay's eye and heart are pierced by splinters falling from the devil's broken mirror, which reflects everything that is beautiful as hideous. It distorts Kay's view of life, and he loses interest in all that is natural and beautiful, even turning on little Gerda. One day when he is out tobogganing he grabs onto the back of a big white sledge to get some speed and comes under the spell of the wicked Snow Queen, who takes him as prisoner to her ice palace in the far north.

No one at home knows what has become of Kay. Eventually everyone assumes he is dead, except little Gerda, who goes looking for him. Her journey is long and treacherous and full of delays, but she never gives up and because of her kindness she makes friends along the way. One of these friends is a reindeer who carries her on his back through Lapland and Finmark, right to the edge of the Snow Queen's frozen garden.

The helpful animal is a common and ancient folklore motif. I particularly like this reindeer, who has just been freed from captivity, and who seems to care almost as much as Gerda about rescuing Kay from his prison.

> ...and the reindeer sped away past brush and briar, through the great forest, over marsh and moor, and the wide plains, as swiftly as he could go. The wolves howled; the ravens screamed; the sky seemed filled with sneezing, crackling noises—schooo, schooo; piff, piff— each time with a glow of red. "Those are my dear old Northern Lights," said the reindeer. "Aren't they beautiful!" Faster and faster he ran, through the night, through the day.... "Schooo, schooo! Crack! crack!" came the noises from the sky, and all night long the glorious Northern Lights flashed violet blue....the reindeer dared not stop; on he ran till he came to the big bush with the red berries. There he put Gerda down, and kissed her on the lips; as he did so, great shining tears ran down the poor animal's face. Then he turned and sped back as fast as he was able. ("The Snow Queen" *Hans Christian Andersen's Fairytales*)

In the palace Gerda finds Kay. He is nearly ice in body and spirit, but she is so relieved at the sight of him that she weeps, and her tears wash the splinters from his heart and eye, releasing him from the Snow Queen's power and the mirror's awful view of life. Then, together on the reindeer and his doe who have returned to wait for them, Gerda and Kay ride home.

KALEVALA—FINLAND

The same year that Hans Christian Andersen published his first book of fairy tales, a Finnish physician named Elias Lonnrot published a book of traditional songs, narrative and magical, sung by the peasant folk in northern Karelia on the Russian border. Lonnrot's aim was to preserve in verse the ancient Finno-Karelian peasant life, a life that was already falling by the wayside.

Lonnrot collected and edited the songs himself and called it *Kalevala: Land of the Heroes.* It came at a time, the mid-nineteenth century, when Finland had produced little in the way of new literature and was also growing restless after centuries of Swedish and then Russian rule. In their struggle to find a national consciousness, the *Kalevala* became a rallying point for the Finnish people, and they took it to their hearts calling it their national epic.

The poems are tied together quite loosely and arbitrarily. There are basically four main characters or heroes: Väinämöinen, Son of the Wind and of the Virgin of the Air, a vigorous old man, patriarch and minstrel; Ilmarinen, his human brother, a handsome young man and great smith and craftsman; Lemminkainen, jovial and reckless, always pulling himself out of a tight place with his magic; and Kullervo, whose tragic history makes him morose and cunning.

Kullervo's story is related in several incidents. In one Kullervo is taken as a slave by a horrible, heartless peasant woman who sends him out to tend her cattle as they graze in the birch forest. To eat she gives him nothing but water and a loaf of bread in which she has baked a stone. Kullervo watches the cattle and grows hungry. Taking out his knife, which is the only keepsake he has left from his family, he cuts into the bread. The knife breaks. Seeing what the wicked peasant woman has done to him, he herds her cattle into a bog, and with his shepherd's horn and magic, he calls the bears and wolves of the forest to follow him back to the farm, where they eat up the wicked woman.

> Then the dusty wicked herd-boy,
> Kullervo, Kalervo's offspring,
> Homeward drove the bears before him,
> And the wolf-flock to the farmyard, . . .

> (Elias Lonnrot, "Kullervo," *Kalevala*)

In Finland the peasant had to be bold and cunning if he were to survive. Certainly this describes Kullervo! This needlework design of the story of Kullervo was inspired by one of a series of ceramic plates illustrating scenes from the *Kalevala,* issued by Arabia Company of Finland.

FAFNISMOL OF THE POETIC EDDA—ICELAND

In the midst of the Viking Age, Norwegians and Irish settled the newly discovered Iceland, and on that barren, isolated island flourished one of the greatest traditions of oral literature in the medieval world, that of the Icelandic skalds—the poet-singers. The sharp-memoried skalds recorded in their minds the stories, mythologies, legends, and songs that had come to Iceland with them from their native lands. They also composed their own works about Icelandic families or foreign kings, whose patronage they gained while traveling abroad. These they passed from generation to generation.

In the Middle Ages, when the written word came to Iceland, the material of the skalds was recorded in nearly the same form as it had first been sung. While languages in other parts of Europe were going through evolutions and great upheavals, leaving much of their preliterate traditions behind and lost forever in the past, the Old Norse language in Iceland remained pure. Indeed, it is much the same language today.

The Poetic Edda or *Elder Edda* is one of the earliest and greatest of the ancient Icelandic manuscripts of oral literature. Set down around the year A.D. 1000, it is the original record of Germanic mythology and heroic legend in their Norse shape. This ancient legend of Germanic heroes, the *Nibelungenlied,* has its beginnings in a time distant even to the Viking Age. The great hero of the legend, Sigfried, or in Norse, Sigurd or Sigurth may even be based on a Frankish warrior of the fifth or sixth century. The poems of the *Poetic Edda* tell the stories of such heroes and heroines as Sigurth, Brynhild, Gudrun, Gunnar, and Atli as the Norse knew them.

The "Fafnismol" is one of those poems. It tells the story of the greatest of Sigurth's heroic deeds, the killing of the dragon Fafnir. There is no battle scene, for Sigurth simply digs a pit in the dragon's usual path to his drinking hole, and when the thirsty Fafnir slithers over it, Sigurth pierces him to the heart with his magic sword, Gram. All this is noted in a short commentary before the actual poem. Then Sigurth leaps from the trench and confronts the dying dragon. The poem is their conversation.

[Fafnir]:
"Youth, oh, youth!   of whom then, youth, art
      thou born?
   Say whose son thou art,
Who in Fafnir's blood   thy bright blade
      reddened,
   And struck thy sword to my heart?"

[Sigurth]:
"The Noble Hart   my name, and I go
   A motherless man abroad;
Father I had not,   as others have,
   And lonely ever I live."

[Fafnir]:
"If father thou hadst not,   as other have,
   By what wonder wast thou born?
(Though thy name on the day   of my death
      thou hidest,
   Thou knowest thou doest lie.)"

[Sigurth]:
"My race, methinks,   is unknown to thee,
   And so am I myself;
Sigurth my name,   and Sigmund's son,
   Who smote thee thus with the sword."

(Bellows, "Fafnismol" *The Poetic Edda*)

Those who know dragon lore tell us that it is a very dangerous thing to tell a dragon your real name, for that can give him power over you. Sigurth obviously knew this and showed his courage with his final honesty. Dragons traditionally can speak, yet this conversation is a particularly fascinating one, for Sigurth seeks the counsel of Fafnir, who is said to be wise in lore.

[Fafnir]:
"I counsel thee, Sigurth,   heed my speech,
   And ride thou homeward hence;
The sounding gold,   the glow-red wealth,
   And the rings thy bane shall be."

[Sigurth]:
"Thy counsel is given,   but go I shall
   To the gold in the heather hidden;
And, Fafnir, thou   with death dost fight,
   Lying where Hel shall have thee."

(Bellows)

Fafnir dies, and Sigurth takes the great treasure the dragon had been hoarding. But Fafnir had spoken true; such ill-gotten treasure is dangerous to mortal man, and ultimately it leads Sigurth to a tragic end.

EAST O' THE SUN AND WEST O' THE MOON—NORWAY

During the same decades that Hans Christian Andersen was writing his fairy tales in Denmark and Elias Lonnrot was collecting his Finno-Karelian songs, two Norwegian men, Peter Christian Asbjørnsen and Jørgen Moe, were setting about to write down the folk stories that had become a part of Norwegian life. It was a rich time for folklore. The Romantic movement had revived interest in it, and folklore became a legitimate occupation. It was fortunate, for oral traditions were dying out, and it is because of folklorists like Asbjørnsen and Moe that they are preserved for us to enjoy today.

One of the stories Asbjørnsen and Moe collected—perhaps the most famous—is "East o' the Sun and West o' the Moon." In the version I like best (and under a different title), a white bear comes to a poor farmer's door one night, offering wealth in return for the peasant's youngest daughter. The farmer talks with his daughter about how greatly it will help their situation, and

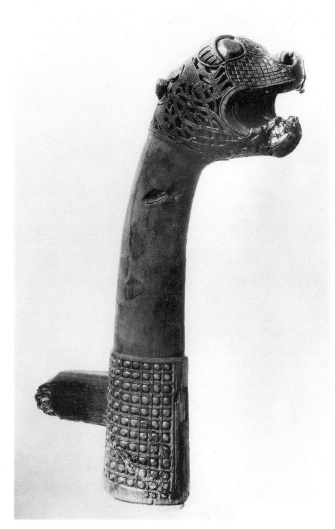

Nineth century carved dragon head, one of two found with the Öseberg Viking ship near Oslo. (Courtesy Universitetet i Oslo Oldsaksamlingen)

she reluctantly agrees. When the bear returns for the answer, she climbs onto his shaggy white back to ride to his home. "'Have you ever sat softer, have you ever seen clearer?' ... 'No, *never*,' she said." (Asbjørnsen and Moe, "White-Bear-King-Valemon" *Norwegian Folktales*)

The bear takes the peasant girl to a castle where she has everything she could want. But a strange event occurs every night: a man comes and lies beside her in the dark. She is not allowed to see him, and by morning light he is gone. When the girl goes home for a visit she tells her mother about this. Her mother gives her a candle to take back with her, telling her to look on the man while he sleeps. When the bear comes to take her back with him, he says, "...if you have listened to your mother's advice, you have brought bad luck on us both, and then, all that has passed between us will be as nothing.'" (Dasent, trans., "East o' the Sun and West o' the Moon")

But that night when the man slept beside her, the peasant girl, unable to resist the temptation, lights her candle and looks upon the man; he is the loveliest prince she has ever seen, and she falls deeply in love with him on the spot. Bending to kiss him, she spills tallow on his shirt and he awakens. " 'What have you done?' he cried; 'now you have made us both unlucky, for had you held out only this one year, I had been freed. But I have a stepmother who has bewitched me, so that I am a White Bear by day, and a Man by night. But now all ties are snapped between us; now I must set off from you to her. She lives in a castle which stands EAST O' THE SUN AND WEST O' THE MOON, and there, too, is a Princess, with a nose three ells long, and she's the wife I must have now.'" (Dasent) In the morning he is gone and the peasant girl sets off to find and rescue him.

THE WONDERFUL ADVENTURES OF NILS—SWEDEN

At the turn of the twentieth century, Selma Lagerlöf was Sweden's greatest living author. When asked to write a geography text for Swedish schoolchildren, she wrote *The Wonderful Adventures of Nils*—a geography text and much more.

I have already quoted from this book quite a bit in Chapter Three. Nils, a cruel, careless boy, is turned into a tiny elf for doing mischief. Before he is even fully aware of his new size, he tries to stop the barnyard gander, Morten, from flying off with a flock of wild geese passing overhead. Nils is accidentally carried away on the migration over the Swedish countryside, from the southernmost province of Skåne to Lapland.

Along the way Nils is cared for by the flock, and especially by the gander, Morten. Their acceptance of him helps Nils realize the shamefulness of his own ways, and he learns to consider others, until he is willing to risk his own life to save the flock from the fox that has stalked them across Sweden.

Nils is a story about growing up: of becoming aware of the sorrow and pain of those around us, as well as their joy. It is coming to see that the whole world is tied together, our sorrow and pain are intertwined, and we each have a part to play in helping if the balance is to be turned to joy.

A person on the back of an animal makes a dramatic picture. Before I even fully realized what I was doing, I had three such scenes—the folklore designs from Denmark, Norway, and Sweden. I have made them the same size and used complementary colors, so they can be a set as well as individual pieces, or they can be stitched together on one long piece of linen or canvas as a frieze.

A MAGIC DRUM SYMBOL—LAPLAND

From as far back as Viking times, Laplanders used magic drums to aid them in making important decisions, to receive answers from their gods, and to heal or harm. Made of wood, magic drums were covered with membranes of reindeer skin on which were painted pictures. There were pictures of the Lapp gods of the forces of nature—sun, snow, wind, thunder—and of the protective spirits of hunting, fishing, and the reindeer herds, and most important of all, those that protected the children and the home. They also drew on the drums reindeer and elk, birds and bears, lakes, rivers, boats, and sledges: a microcosmic map of the Lapp world.

When an answer was needed to a problem of any kind, the Lapp shaman could consult his drum. Sometimes he used a small piece of horn or bone as an indicator. It would move over the different figures on the membrane as he beat the drum until it settled on a painted symbol, in essence telling a story, which the shaman interpreted for an answer to the question. In this way the wandering Lapps,

1. *Lapp magic drum reindeer from rubbings made by Ernst Manker.*

by carrying their drums with them, could take their gods with them wherever they went and communicate with them and receive their help. When Christianity came, the priests sought out the magic drums and burned them because they were pagan. Only about eighty drums survived, and these are now in museums.[7]

For his book, *People of Eight Seasons, The Story of the Lapps,* Ernst Manker traced a number of the reindeer from the surviving drums and sent them running over the endpapers as decoration. Set in this way, the reindeer of the Lapp magic drums evoke the primitive animals on the Överhogdal textile from twelfth-century Sweden, or the drawings on Stone Age caves. These reindeer are powerful and graceful in their primitive simplicity. Out of the tracings, I chose three reindeer and translated them into patterns for counted thread embroidery.

Chapter Five

General Instructions for Counted Thread Embroidery

This chapter includes instructions for techniques and materials used throughout the book. It is advisable to read through this chapter completely before beginning any projects.

Counted thread embroidery is worked on an unmarked ground. Each stitch is counted individually, working from a pattern on graph paper. In this way the pattern can be used more than once and in different materials and sizes. A counted thread project may be all one color—monochromatic—or it may be a spray of color like a spring bouquet.

Counted thread embroidery can be worked in any stitch that uses a cross-stitch-style graphic pattern. For this book I have chosen four counted thread stitches that are common in Scandinavia: cross-stitch, long-armed cross-stitch, double cross-stitch, and upright *gobelin* stitch. Each has played a part in the history of Scandinavian embroidery and continues to enjoy popularity in Scandinavia today.

Needleworkers will probably never agree about how all the steps of counted thread embroidery should be executed. Some people are purists; they are interested in preserving traditions, and they endeavor to follow techniques and patterns exactly. Others need room to be creative; they find absolute rules constricting and prefer to take them rather as general guidelines. One of these ways preserves tradition, the other makes new traditions.

I believe that personality more than anything else determines your preference. If you become aware of what suits you best, then you can choose that particular route for doing needlework. Approach embroidery in the way that most satisfies you, for one thing seems certain: if you do not enjoy it, there is no point in doing it, and you probably will not.

Choosing and Changing Materials

Each of the designs in this book has been embroidered in a sample piece, which is shown in the color photographs. Most of the designs can also be worked in other counted thread stitches and materials as well as those used to make the samples (see charts 3, 4, and 5 in the Appendix). There is versatility in the different articles each design can make, too; for instance, the designs for the yokes of the little girls' jumpers can be used as borders for table runners or tray liners. With the instructions in Chapter Six, I suggest at least one alternative set of materials for each design, but that by no means exhausts the possibilities. If I have not suggested what you would like in the way of colors or materials, you may wish to plan the materials yourself.

Basically, there is one major choice: you can stitch a design on appropriate counted thread fabric with appropriate threads, or you can work it on canvas with wools. On canvas the entire piece, including the background, must be filled in with stitching. This is not the case with fabric, where the background or parts of the design may be left open, making the fabric an integral part of the overall picture. To be sure, a few of the designs work only on fabric, but even then there are options about what kind of counted thread fabric, thread, and stitch you may wish to use. Types of threads include cotton embroidery floss, cotton flower thread, linen thread, and separable wools, the latter of which are used on even-weave wool or very fine canvas. Counted thread fabrics include linen, cotton aida, wool, and a variety of synthetics and synthetic/natural blends.

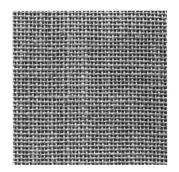

Finely woven linen.

Coarse linen.

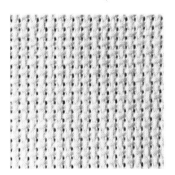

Aida cloth.

Penelope canvas.

To help you decide on materials, you might first consider how and where the finished needlework will be used. This will give you an idea of size, which in turn will help you choose between canvas and fabric. Canvas and wool needlework tends to be quite a bit larger than the same design worked on finer fabrics. For instance, the design of the Norwegian tale, "East o' the Sun and West o' the Moon," is 16 x 21 inches on canvas, and only 6 x 8½ inches on fine linen. Consider: do you want to fill a wall or only a small space? How big is the table if you are making a table runner? Do you want a throw pillow for a couch or chair? Do you have a long narrow space to fill? Perhaps putting two or three designs together on one piece of fabric would work—dolls or the matching folktales, for instance.

Once you have mapped out your project, use charts 1 and 2 to calculate the size your finished work will be. Chart 1 interprets the different counted thread fabrics and canvas in terms of how many stitches they hold per inch. Chart 2 lists the width and length, in stitches, of each design in this book. To figure out how large any design will be in any one fabric, divide the numbers in the left margin of chart 2 by the appropriate figure from chart 1. For example, the Homestead Collection's Norseman Sampler is 251 stitches tall by 178 stitches wide. If you choose to stitch it on 28 count linen (which chart 1 tells you holds 14 stitches to the inch), you would work this equation: 251 ÷ 14 = 18 inches tall and 178 ÷ 14 = 13 inches wide. The design will be 18 inches x 13 inches on

28 count linen.

Chart 2 works some of these mathematics for you for the most common sizes of counted thread

Chart 1. Number of stitches per inch for even-weave fabrics.

Size	Linen and all linen weaves	Aida and all aida weaves	Penelope canvas
6 count		6	
8 count		8	
9 count		9	5
10 count		10	5½
11 count		11	6
12 count	6	12	6½
14 count	7	14	7½
15 count	7½	15	
18 count	9	18	
20 count	10	20	
22 count	11	22	
24 count	12		
26 count	13		
27 count	13½		
28 count	14		
30 count	15		

Note: "Count" refers to number of threads or holes in the fabric per inch. It is not necessarily the number of stitches that fabric will hold per inch. For aida and fabrics woven like aida, stitching is over 1 square, and thus the count equals the number of stitches per inch. But for linen-style weaves, stitching is over 2 threads, so the count is twice the number of stitches per inch.

Chart 2. Dimensions for designs, length by width.

Number of stitches:	Design	Approximate finished size on fabric with:		
		14 stitches per inch	11 stitches per inch	5 stitches per inch
	The Homestead Collection			
251 x 178	Norseman Sampler	18 in. x 13 in.	23 in. x 16 in.	50 in. x 35 in.
285 x 189	The Lord's Prayer Sampler	21 in. x 14 in.	26 in. x 17 in.	57 in. x 38 in.
151 x 107	Baby's Room Sampler	11 in. x 7 in.	14 in. x 10 in.	30 in. x 21 in.
* x 119	Table Runner	* x 8 in.	* x 11 in.	* x 23 in.
191 x 35	Bellpull	2½ in. x 13 in.	3 in. x 17 in.	7 in. x 38 in.
78 x 77	Farm Couple Picture	5 in. x 5 in.	7½ in. x 7½ in.	15 in. x 15 in.
81 x 91	Sheep Picture	6 in. x 6 in.	7 in. x 8 in.	16 in. x 18 in.
64 x 92	Chickens Picture	4 in. x 6 in.	6 in. x 8 in.	13 in. x 18 in.
136 x 50	Gudbrandsdal Man	10 in. x 3 in.	12 in. x 4 in.	27 in. x 10 in.
130 x 58	Gudbrandsdal Woman	9 in. x 4 in.	11 in. x 5 in.	26 in. x 11 in.
46 x 82	Sheep Doll	3 in. x 6 in.	4 in. x 7 in.	9 in. x 16 in.
16 x 210	Sheep Place Mat	1 in. x 15 in.	1½ in. x 19 in.	—
16 x 16	Sheep Napkin/Breadcloth	2 in. x 2 in.	2½ in. x 2½ in.	—
65 x 65	Tray Liner	6 in. x 6 in.	8 in. x 8 in.	14 in. x 14 in.
16 x 29	Sheep Bib	1 in. x 2 in.	1½ in. x 2½ in.	3 in. x 6 in.
18 x 13	Chick Bib	1 in. x 1 in.	1½ in. x 1½ in.	3 in. x 3 in.
16 x 107	Sheep Jumper	1 in. x 7 in.	—	—
95 x 73	Rosemaling Snapshot Frames	7 in. x 5 in.	—	—
	The Snowflake Collection			
* x 207	Table Runner	* x 15 in.	* x 19 in.	* x 41 in.
189 x 47	Bellpull	13 in. x 3 in.	17 in. x 4 in.	38 in. x 10 in.
47 x 47	Snowflake Pictures (3)	3 in. x 3 in.	4 in. x 4 in.	10 in. x 10 in.
13 x 208	Snowflake Place Mat	1 in. x 15 in.	1½ in. x 19 in.	—
13 x 13	Snowflake Napkin/Breadcover	2 in. x 2 in.	2½ in. x 2½ in.	—
65 x 65	Tray Liner	6 in. x 6 in.	8 in. x 8 in.	14 in. x 14 in.
25 x 23	Reindeer Bib	1½ in. x 1½ in.	2 in. x 2 in.	5 in. x 5 in.
25 x 103	Reindeer Jumper	2 in. x 7 in.	—	—
27 x 24	Gift Bag	2 in. x 2 in.	2½ in. x 2½ in.	5 in. x 5 in.
15 x 15	Tree Decorations	1 in. x 1 in.	1½ in. x 1½ in.	3 in. x 3 in.
	Bits of Christmas			
100 x 61	Reindeer Stocking	7 in. x 4 in.	9 in. x 6 in.	20 in. x 12 in.
100 x 61	St. Lucia Stocking	7 in. x 4 in.	9 in. x 6 in.	20 in. x 12 in.
* x 95	Lucia Bride Table Runner	* x 6½ in.	* x 8 in.	* x 19 in.
113 x 29	Lucia Bride Bellpull	8 in. x 2 in.	10 in. x 2½ in.	22 in. x 6 in.
63 x 81	Lucia Bride Picture	4 in. x 6 in.	6 in. x 8 in.	12 in. x 16 in.
76 x 60	Bethlehem Scene	5 in. x 4 in.	7 in. x 5 in.	15 in. x 12 in.
	The Folklore Collection			
110 x 80	The Snow Queen	8 in. x 6 in.	10 in. x 7 in.	22 in. x 16 in.
55 x 99	Kalevala	4 in. x 7 in.	5 in. x 9 in.	11 in. x 20 in.
130 x 299	Fafnismol	9 in. x 21 in.	12 in. x 27 in.	26 in. x 60 in.
110 x 80	East o' the Sun	8 in. x 6 in.	10 in. x 7 in.	22 in. x 16 in.
110 x 80	The Won. Adv. of Nils	8 in. x 6 in.	10 in. x 7 in.	22 in. x 16 in.
132 x 150	Magic Drum Symbol 1	9 in. x 11 in.	12 in. x 13 in.	26 in. x 30 in.
118 x 129	Magic Drum Symbol 2	8½ in. x 9 in.	11 in. x 12 in.	23½ in. x 26 in.
126 x 129	Magic Drum Symbol 3	9 in. x 8½ in.	11½ in. x 11 in.	25 in. x 24 in.

*May be made any length desired.

Number of stitches:	Design	Doll height on fabric with:			
		14 stitches per inch	11 stitches per inch	7½ stitches per inch	5 stitches per inch
	Folk Costume Collection				
128 x 45	Hedebo Man	9 in.	11½ in.	17 in.	25 in.
119 x 44	Hedebo Woman	8½ in.	11 in.	16 in.	24 in.
131 x 47	Karelian Man	9½ in.	12 in.	17 in.	26 in.
119 x 41	Karelian Woman	8½ in.	11 in.	16 in.	24 in.
116 x 43	Icelandic Woman	8 in.	10½ in.	15½ in.	23 in.
124 x 45	Hardanger Man	9 in.	11 in.	16½ in.	25 in.
116 x 47	Hardanger Woman	8 in.	10½ in.	15½ in.	23 in.
124 x 48	Hälsingland Man	9 in.	11 in.	16½ in.	25 in.
116 x 56	Hälsingland Woman	8 in.	10½ in.	15½ in.	23 in.
75 x 39	Dalarna Girl	5½ in.	7 in.	10 in.	15 in.
115 x 56	Finmark Woman	8 in.	10½ in.	15½ in.	23 in.
78 x 31	Finmark Boy	5½ in.	7 in.	10½ in.	15½ in.

Note: Dolls will be approximately half as wide as they are tall.
The dimensions given here are finished sizes. Add 4 to 6 inches to these figures to determine the cut size of your piece of fabric.

fabric. They are listed in the columns to the right in chart 2. These are dimensions for the finished sizes of the designs, not the size the material should be cut. Four to 6 inches should be added to each of the dimensions to arrive at the size of material to be cut. (Add 4 inches for small designs less than 6 inches square, 6 inches for everything bigger.) For example, for the Norseman Sampler above: 18 + 6 = 24 and 13 + 6 = 19. The size of the material you should buy is 24 inches x 19 inches.

Supplies

Counted thread supplies can be purchased in any needlework store, many fabric stores, and some Scandinavian gift shops. Although a wide range of quality (and prices) is available, think twice before trading quality for bargain prices. You will be investing a lot of your time and energy into these projects, and you want them to be durable and enduring. Bargain material may not hold up over the years. Bargain fabric, once embroidered, may not even block out square in the end, so that

all the effort is wasted. Several of the better quality counted thread materials available as of this writing are listed in the Appendix. There are many good quality counted thread supplies on the market and new ones are being manufactured all the time, so consult with your shopkeeper about what is available. Ask to check the material for flaws before it is cut. See chart 4 in the Appendix for ideas on matching threads and wools to fabrics.

Test wash any thread you suspect might bleed. Some reds and darker colored threads have excess dyestuffs that the manufacturer may suggest rinsing out before using.

Equipment

The only essential piece of equipment for counted thread embroidery is a blunt tapestry needle. A blunt needle slides neatly into the holes of counted thread fabric while a sharp needle will catch and split the threads of the material. For fine fabrics (13 stitches to the inch or more) use tapestry needle size 24 or 26. For coarse fabrics (11 or fewer stitches to the inch) use tapestry needle number 22. When working with penelope canvas and wool use a size 18 or 20 needle.

Some people like to use embroidery hoops or stretcher frames. These can be especially helpful for those who tend to pull their threads too tightly, puckering the material. Stretcher bars and hoops give a counter pull to such a too tight stitch. If you use a hoop, remove it when you are not stitching, as it can pull any fabric, and especially linen, permanently out of shape. Fabric can be left on a stretcher frame with no harm.

Good lighting is essential for needlework. By daylight I work next to a large expanse of south-facing windows. By night I sit close to a three-way lamp turned on bright. Some people require magnification, and there are special magnifying glasses and stands manufactured for embroiderers. It is an old wives' tale that embroidering can ruin eyesight. If you work in good light and quit when your eyes begin to grow tired, there should be no problem.

Preparing the Fabric

If you have chosen to stitch on linen, aida, or synthetic cloth, first protect the edges from unraveling by machine zigzagging or serging all the way around. If you are planning to use a stretcher bar, you may chose instead to baste double-fold bias tape around the edges, which you can sew in turn onto the stretcher bar tabs. Never use chemicals, glues, or tape to prevent ravelling; it is not known what long-term effects these might have on the material and embroidery.

Threading Needles

Cut your thread or wool yarn a maximum of 18 inches long. Longer strands tend to wear as they are pulled through the holes, getting dull and thin. If you are using embroidery floss, strip the thread first to break the static charge left by manufacturing processes. To do this, separate all 6 strands, then put 2 (or as many as you will be embroidering with) back together again. Static charge causes thread to catch and tangle more easily, as does threading a needle with the wrong end of the thread. Threads and yarns have naps to them; the fibers have been spun in one direction just as a cat's fur grows one way. Embroidering with the nap backwards is like petting a cat the wrong way; instead of laying smooth, fibers go in all directions. To embroider with the nap, thread the first end off the skein through the needle, or thread the needle first before cutting the thread off the skein.

Thread your embroidery floss, linen thread, or cotton flower thread through a needle as you do sewing thread. Thick and fluffy yarn threads best when an end of yard is looped over the eye of the needle, pulled tight, and then pulled off the needle and pressed through its eye. Bring the needle toward the stationary thread.

Centering

Unless instructed otherwise, begin counted thread embroidery in the center. To find center, fold the fabric lengthwise then widthwise or count individual threads top to bottom and side to side, finding their intersection. It is often useful to run a basting stitch along both of these lines in a contrasting sewing thread for reference. You may wish to mark the same lines on the pattern with a yellow highlighter. Arrows in the margins of each pattern point to the center of the design. These reference lines can help you keep your count accurate. With samplers, run basting lines down each side for reference. If your basting line runs every 10 threads on linen weaves or 5 squares on aida weaves (over 5, under 5, etc.), it can be used rather than having to count individual stitches all of the time.

Anchoring Threads

Knots are not used in counted thread embroidery. They pucker the fabric, make bumps underneath when the work is ironed, and often show through as distracting masses. To anchor the starting thread, come through the back of the cloth, holding a tail of thread or yarn about the length of your needle in the back with your fingers. Then take a few stitches, each time catching the tail thread and sewing it down as you go.

To anchor the end of a thread, run it under the reverse side of four or five stitches and clip the excess. Subsequent threads can be anchored in this same way or as the first thread was anchored.

Tension

Tension is a key element of counted thread. Too much tension distorts fabric, making holes and puckers. Stitching that is too loose looks sloppy. For correct tension, pull gently on the thread just until there is resistance from the fabric, no more. A too tight stitch can be alleviated by using a hoop or stretcher frame as counter tension.

Sewing Versus Poking

I have observed two kinds of embroiderers. Pokers push their needle down, reach under the fabric to pull it through and push it back up, then bring their hand back to the top of the fabric and repeat the process. Or they use a needlework stand, which frees both hands so that one can be above and one under the cloth working. Sewers push their needle down and back up in the next hole all in one movement, using just one hand and keeping it on top of the fabric the whole time. Many purists argue that poking is the correct method. It certainly is a good way for beginners to start. Thread tends to lie flat more readily with a poking technique, and there is less chance of catching and splitting threads.

You will probably simply find you prefer one technique over the other. It has a lot to do with finding the rhythm of each stitch as it works best for you. Let it be relaxing and enjoyable.

Embroidering

Begin each row in the far holes and stitch toward what you have already embroidered, rather than bringing your thread up through the holes that already have been partially filled with the previous row's threads (see fig. 2). This way, if you split or damage the previous stitch, it will only show on the back side of the embroidery. Work all of the counted thread stitches first. French knots and backstitches for outlining should be stitched last, as finishing touches.

Straighten the thread periodically by holding the embroidery upside down and dangling the needle so that it can spin out of any twists. Twisted thread will not lie flat. This is especially important with upright *gobelin* stitch, which has a satin look.

2. *Stitch toward your finished stitching.*

When stitching in several colors, it is sometimes handy to thread several needles, one with each color, to use as needed. They can be kept organized and at hand on a magnetic needle holder.

Washing, Blocking, and Ironing

Counted thread materials absorb oil and dirt while they are being stitched. These can cause discoloration if they are not washed out. A gentle but thorough washing by hand will freshen up the material and even help the stitching lie better. Do this before the embroidery is framed, mounted, or sewn. (Also remember to preshrink any fabrics you plan to use as backing or to make pillows, baskets, or clothing.)

Unless the manufacturer suggests otherwise, first soak embroidery for an hour in cold water. This will remove any excess dye without causing it to bleed into the fabric. Rinse in several batches of cold water, then wash the work using a mild soap (never detergent) in cold or tepid water. Rinse it three or four times in cold water.

Remove the excess water after rinsing by pressing the embroidery between several towels. Never wring or roll it. Lay it flat on a dry towel and block it out by pulling on corners and sides until it is square. Cover it with another towel and let it dry out of direct sunlight and at room temperature.

If the embroidery requires more blocking, use rustproof straight pins and a porous surface such as heavy cardboard, cork, or even carpet. Lay a smooth, wet towel on the board with the embroidery right side up over that. Pin each corner, stretching the embroidery and squaring it. Then pin the middle of each side, always stretching to square. Add more pins until they are close together all around the embroidery, pulling the material where necessary. Leave it to dry at room temperature, which may take several days. Then leave it one day longer to help prevent it from pulling back out of shape.

Iron embroidery facedown on a padded surface (3 or 4 towels work well). Spread a piece of moistened muslin or other thin material over it and iron until dry. Then iron the embroidery directly until it is dry. Never iron the right side of needlework as that flattens and distorts the stitches.

Care and Storage

All natural counted thread embroidery materials have some natural moisture and therefore need to breathe. Airtight containers can cause them to rot or mildew. If you store your working embroidery in a plastic bag, first punch holes in the bag. Never use chemicals on needlework, as their effects over the years are not certain. Sealants or water and stain repellants are undesirable since they do not allow the materials to breathe. Hang and display embroidery where it will not be faded by hot, direct sunlight. (See the end of this chapter for information on framing.)

Clean your needlework as needed. Most needlework needs only an occasional vacuuming to remove dust. Embroidery hung in a kitchen or bath may require washing every few years.

The Stitches

CROSS-STITCH

Denmark: *korssting*
Finland: *ristipisto*
Iceland: *krosssaumurin*
Norway: *korssting*
Sweden: *korsstygn*

Cross-stitch consists of perpendicular diagonal strokes creating an "x." It can be worked one of two ways: either complete each individual stitch as you go (see fig. 3) or stitch a row of strokes going one way then come back the other way crossing them (see fig. 4). The second method is particularly good for long rows and large areas of fill-in, and for me the thread lies down more smoothly using this method.

Each cross equals 1 square on a pattern. Stitches should cross in the same direction (fig. 5); this gives a neater appearance. On linen weave fabrics, sew over 2 threads, on aida weaves embroider over 1 square.

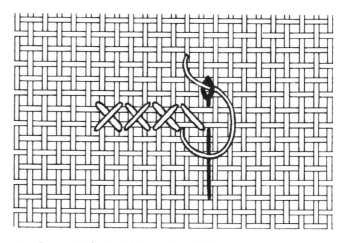

3. *Cross-stitch, finishing each stitch as you go.*

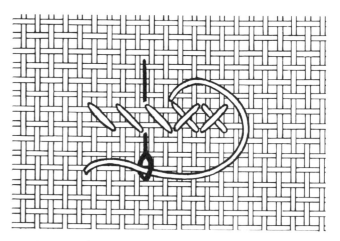

4. *Cross-stitch, running stitches one way and crossing on the return.*

Cross-stitch.

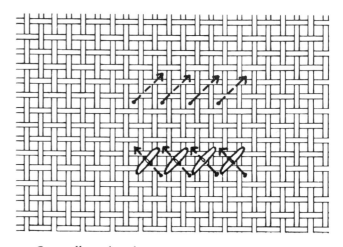

5. *Cross all stitches the same way.*

Long-armed cross-stitch.

LONG-ARMED CROSS-STITCH

Denmark: *flettesting*
Swedish Finland: *tvistsöm*
Iceland: *gamli krosssaumurinn*
Norway: *twistsøm*
Sweden: *tvistsöm*

Long-armed cross-stitch alternates 1 regular length cross-stitch stroke (over 2 threads or 1 square) with 1 long cross-stroke (over 4 threads or 2 squares). (See fig. 6a.) It is worked alternately, first a row from left to right, then a row returning from right to left. The first and last stitches in a

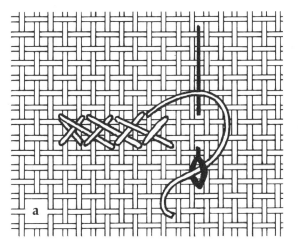
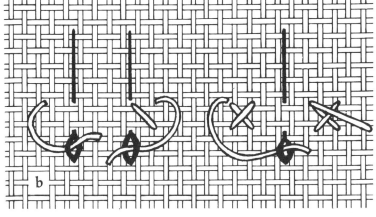

6. *Long-armed cross-stitch.*

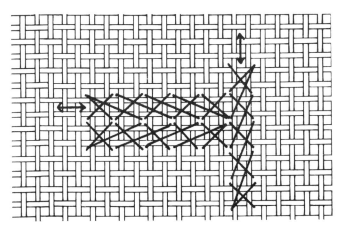

7. *Long-armed cross-stitch worked horizontally and vertically.*

row are anchored with a complete cross-stitch (2 short stroked over the long one, see fig. 6b).

Long-armed cross-stitch has an especially nice rhythm, soothing and meditative. Yet at the same time it stitches up very rapidly. It is a heavily textured stitch. The Danish word for it, *flettesting*, means "braid stitch," and indeed it looks braided. Many rows of it give a linear effect, which follows the direction of stitching—horizontal if stitching back and forth, vertical if stitching up and down. If the figures in a design are worked one way and the background the opposite, it makes the figures stand out nicely. This is how the samples of the folktales in long-armed cross-stitch have been stitched (see fig. 7).

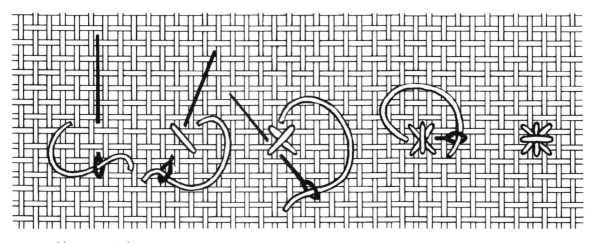

8. *Double cross-stitch.*

DOUBLE CROSS-STITCH

Denmark: *smyrna*
Finland: *kaksoisristipisto*
Norway: *diamondsting*
Sweden: *smyrna*

Double cross-stitch is the slowest of the 4 counted thread stitches described in this book, because it uses 4 complete strokes to make each stitch. Its rhythm is calm and restful.

Double cross-stitch is bulky, so it works best on canvas that is at least 9 count or larger, or on linen weaves with no more than 13 stitches per inch. Because of its nature, double cross-stitch does not work on aida weaves. The texture is lovely: thick, padded, and starlike. The Norwegians call it "diamond stitch."

Each double cross-stitch equals 1 square on a pattern. Try to layer the 4 strokes that make up each double cross-stitch the same way every time, making the "x" first and then the "+." To contrast the background from the figures in the design, put the horizontal stroke of the "+" on top for one (either figure or background) and the vertical stroke on top for the other (see fig. 8).

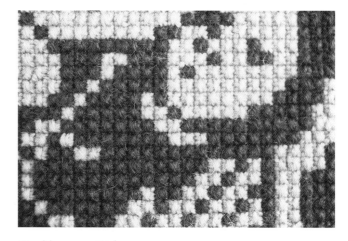

Double cross-stitch.

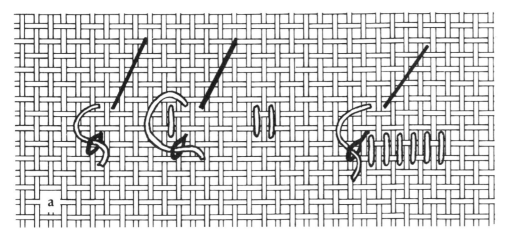

9. *Upright gobelin stitch.*

10. *Completed stitches of two versions of gobelin.*

UPRIGHT *GOBELIN* STITCH

Denmark: *gobelin*
Finland: *laakapisto*
Iceland: *glitsaumur* (straight darning)
Norway: *klostersøm*
Sweden: *gobelin*

Gobelin stitch is very different from the other three counted thread stitches in this book. They are all crossed stitches, but with *gobelin* there is no crossing. Rather the strokes are laid side by side. *Gobelin* may be vertical, diagonal, horizontal, or sometimes mixed. In Scandinavia it is most commonly all laid vertically or upright. The long smooth rows have a striped look when they are all completed (see fig. 9).

To achieve the desired satin look of the finished piece, it is especially important to keep the yarn straight and smooth as you work with it, as well as to begin each stitch away from the previously stitched row and then finish the stitch into the previous row so that threads are not split. Upright *gobelin* is usually worked in wools on canvas. It is most commonly either 3 stitches over 3 double threads of the canvas per square on the

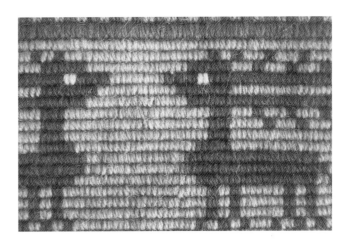

Upright gobelin *stitch.*

pattern (fig. 10a), or 2 stitches over 2 threads of the canvas per square on the pattern (fig. 10b).

Gobelin stitch relaxes like gently flowing water. It takes very little conscious thought, so it is great for letting your mind wander.

Other Embroidery Stitches

BACKSTITCH

The backstitch is used for outlining where needed or for making short stems and leaves. It is also a strong stitch for sewing the dolls together (see fig. 11).

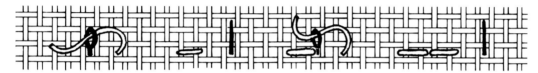

11. *Backstitch.*

WEAVESTITCH

This decorative stitch runs around the edges of place mats, napkins, and breadcloths (see fig. 12).

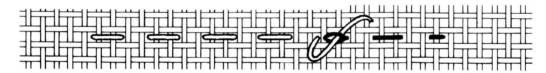

12. *Weavestitch (also known as running stitch).*

FRENCH KNOT

The French knot is used for making eyes. Wrap the thread around the needle twice then insert the needle close to, but not exactly where the thread first emerged (see fig. 13).

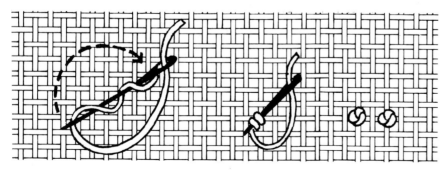

13. *French knot.*

Other Sewing Stitches

SLIP STITCH

This is an invisible stitch for closing pillows and dolls, etc. (see fig. 14).

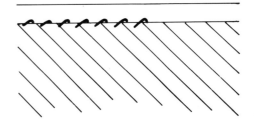

14. *Slip stitch.*

BASTING STITCH

These long running stitches are used to mark the center on counted thread fabric (see fig. 15).

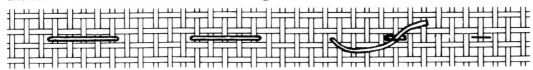

15. *Basting stitch.*

HEMSTITCH

The hemstitch is one way to finish the edges of embroidery. It is most commonly used as the edging for doilies, tablecloths, and place mats made of linen, where the threads are sometimes drawn tight to create a pattern of holes along the edge. However, it can also be used with aida and synthetic materials and the threads not drawn. Hemstitch is usually sewn over 3 threads on linen, although it may be over 2 to 4 stitches depending on the size and firmness of the fabric.

First fold the fabric as directed for making corners (below). Sewing from the back, sew 1 stitch over 3 threads beginning in the fore hole and ending in the rear hole so your thread crosses itself on the wrong side of the fabric. Then take a little stitch in the hem (fig. 16a). Repeat all around the hem. Each stitch over 3 threads can be pulled tight, drawing the threads together and making a neat row of holes along the edge (fig. 16b), or it can be worked without drawing the thread (see fig. 16c). All of the samplers in this book have been hemstitched, then sewn to another piece of linen, stretched, and framed.

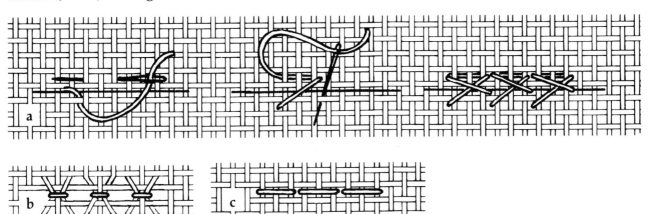

16. *Hemstitch.*

Corners

Corners for a hemstitched edge can be mitered or straight. For a mitered corner, cut a diagonal piece off the corner ½ inch from the intended corner point (fig. 17a). Fold this diagonal edge back ½ inch to the corner (fig. 17b). Then fold the two edges on either side down twice so the two edges meet, forming a pointed corner (fig. 17c and d). Slip-stitch these edges together. Then hemstitch the entire hem.

Straight corners are easier and should be used when there is very little selvage. To make a straight corner, cut a rectangle of excess material out of the corner (fig. 18a). Turn down the side with the short arm of the rectangle twice (fig. 18b). Hemstitch. Then turn in the side with the long arm of the rectangle so it laps over the side just hemstitched (fig. 18c). Hemstitch, hiding the stitches that run up to the top of the corner by slip-stitching them so they do not show through to the front (fig. 18d).

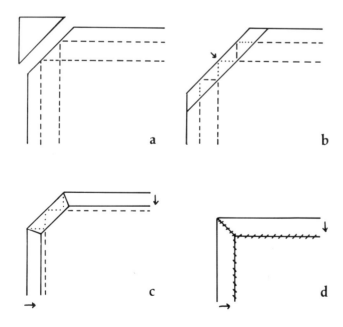

17. *Mitered corner.*

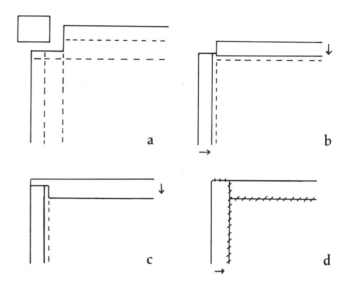

18. *Straight corner.*

Finishing Projects

BELLPULL

Use preshrunk muslin or cotton for the backing. Fold bellpull back evenly on both sides to width desired. Press. Cut backing ½ inch wider and 1 inch shorter than bellpull. Fold backing under ½ inch on both sides and ½ inch on top and bottom. Press. Centering backing on bellpull, wrong sides together, slip-stitch along the sides. Fold bellpull over backing at top and bottom. Fold under ½ inch. Press. Slip-stitch. Insert fittings. Bottom may be fringed, if desired.

MINIBELLPULL, BOOKMARK, OR BELT ON RIBBAND

Use a second piece of Ribband, the same length for backing material. For extra stiffness sew interfacing to the inside of the backing. With right sides together match edge scallops and slip-stitch embroidery to backing along both sides. To finish ends press both pieces to inside ½ inch. Insert fittings or buckles if appropriate. Slip-stitch securely.

SAMPLER

Frame using mattes or hemstitch according to instructions on page 67. Use fittings if desired or sew onto a large piece of matching counted thread fabric and frame.

WALL HANGING

Back according to the instructions for the bellpull or hemstitch according to instructions on page 67, or frame.

Note: For backing a canvas and wool wall hanging, make the backing the same size as the hanging.

TABLE RUNNER

Back according to the instructions for the bellpull. Fringe both ends.

BREADCLOTH, NAPKIN, PLACE MAT

Use linen, aida, salem, or other 13 to 15 stitches per inch fabric for these pieces. Before working the embroidery sew a machine stitch all the way around the fabric in matching thread, 12 threads from the edge, turning square corners. Fringe. An alternative is to hemstitch according to instructions on page 67 after embroidering. Or you can buy the breadcloth, napkin, or place mat ready-made.

Here are suggested fabric cut sizes: place mat 13 inches x 18½ inches; small napkin 12 inches x 12 inches; large napkin 14 inches x 14 inches; small breadcloth 16 inches x 16 inches; large breadcloth 18 inches x 18 inches.

DOLL

Use an identical piece of counted thread fabric for the backing. Press each piece. With right sides together sew together by backstitching through both layers, ⅝ inch to ¾ inch from the edge of the embroidery as seen from the wrong side. Make all curves and turns shallow and round. Leave bottom open. Trim selvage around stitching to ½ inch. Clip curves. Turn and press lightly, pushing out all curves. Fill with batting such as polyfill. Turn under edges on bottom and slip-stitch.

TREE DECORATION

Using colored satin backing, back and fill the decorations according to instructions for the dolls. Slip a loop of thread through top and tie for hanging. As an alternative, you can frame the decorations with small frames from an embroidery supply store.

GIFT BAG

Fold the bag in half lengthwise so that right sides are together. Backstitch along both sides, ½ inch from edge. Turn and press lightly. Fringe the top ½ inch. Cut a piece of floss about 16 inches long. Using 4 strands weavestitch around top, ½ inch from edge. Pull long ends even and use as a tie.

CHRISTMAS STOCKING

For thread embroidery, use satin or matching counted thread fabric for the backing. For wool and canvas embroidery, use corduroy or wool (may be cut from an old pair of trousers) for the backing. Line the stocking with satin or sateen. Cut the selvage of the stocking to ⅝ inch from embroidery edge. Cut the backing to match. Cut 2 pieces of lining, right sides together, the same size and shape as the stocking. With right sides together sew the stocking to backing around edges, leaving top open. Turn and press. Press under top selvages. Make a loop, about 3 inches long and 1 inch to 2 inches wide, of the backing material. Sew a loop firmly to selvage of backing and across fold; loop up as if for hanging (fig. 19a). With right sides together sew the two pieces of lining together around the edges, leaving top open (fig. 19b). Press the top edges out ¾ inch all the way around. Insert the lining, wrong side out, into the stocking. Adjust, matching the

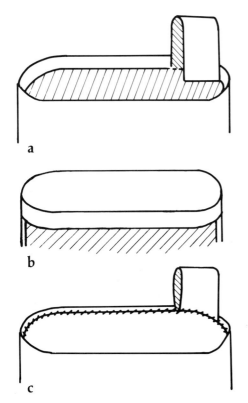

19. *Christmas stocking.*

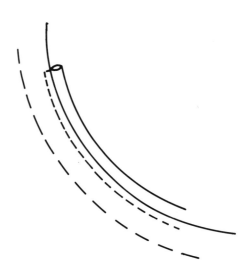

20. *Placement of piping on bib.*

seams and the top edges. Slip-stitch lining to the stocking all around the top edge (fig. 19c).

BIB

Use preshrunk, light cotton such as muslin for the backing. Use piping and double-fold bias tape in matching colors for the trim. Trace the pattern in the Appendix onto tissue paper. Cut the bib to pattern shape, carefully centering the embroidered design. Cut a backing to match. Pin the piping, selvage out, to outside edges of right side of the bib, at seam line (see fig. 20). Baste. With right sides together, sew the bib to the backing around the outside edge on the seam line. Turn at neck opening and press. Cut double-fold bias tape 24 inches to 30 inches longer than the neck opening (for ties). Pin bias tape to the neck edge, matching centers and catching the neck edge inside the fold of the tape. Sew the neck edge. Then sew again all along the bias tape, folding in the ends.

LITTLE GIRLS' JUMPER

The jumper is a Simplicity pattern available in sizes 3 to 6 at any fabric store. Full instructions are included with the pattern. Cut the yoke of counted thread material (13 to 14 stitches per inch). Zigzag or serge the edges. Embroider it before sewing the jumper.

PILLOW

Use wool, corduroy, linen-look, or heavy cotton material for pillow. You will also need a pillow form or batting. The zipper is optional. Pillows may have pleated corners, ruffles, or piping trim around the edges. Cut 2 identical pieces of fabric for front and back, adding 1 inch to desired length and width for seams. (The pillows in this book are 12 inches to 14 inches finished size.) Trim embroidery ½ inch longer and wider than desired size. Turn under ¼ inch on all sides and press. Center the embroidery right side up on right side of pillow front. Pin. Add lace or trim if desired. Slip-stitch in place. If a zipper is desired sew in according to packaging instructions. Make ruffle, pleated corners, or piping and sew on according to instructions below. Machine stitch around pillow, leaving a 6- to 9-inch opening at the bottom if there is no zipper. Turn and press. Insert pillow form or batting. Slip-stitch opening if there is no zipper. Note: a pillow form can be made by sewing together 2 pieces of muslin slightly larger than the pillow and filling loosely with polyfill.

For pleated corners: with right sides together and before sewing back to front, clip points off corners leaving a 2- to 3-inch diagonal. Fold 3 to 4 pleats across each diagonal. Continue as above, sewing through the pleats (see fig. 21).

For ruffle: cut the ruffle of matching material 3 inches to 4 inches wide and 1½ times the circumference of the pillow. Fold in half length-wise. Press. Machine baste using a long stitch, ½ inch from raw edge then again ¼ inch from edge. Gather to fit around the pillow. Pin ruffle to the pillow front, right sides together. Baste. Pin the pillow front to back and continue as above.

For piping: pin piping, raw edge out, around the seam line of the front of the pillow, beginning in the center of the bottom edge and overlapping piping ½ inch. Baste. Pin the pillow front to back and sew together on that same seam.

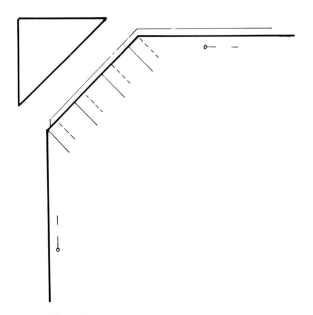

21. *Pleated corners.*

BASKET

Select a basket and enough cotton fabric to line it and make a cover for it. Cut cover for the basket about 1½ inches wider and longer than the lip of the basket. Sew just as for ruffle pillow, using a sheet of quilt batting or a piece of needle punch as fill. Line the basket by cutting one large oval or round-cornered rectangle that fits around the whole basket—under it, up the sides, and over the lip about 1 inch. Turn under ½ inch and hem. Then zigzag over a piece of small cord elastic placed on that same hem line and cut ½ inch to 1 inch longer than the circumference of the basket. Stretch it to fit all the way around the edge of the fabric. Line the basket with this piece, the elastic edge turned over the lip of the basket. Baskets with handles must have their lining glued in.

PICTURE FRAME

Use identical counted thread fabric for the backing. You will also need: a piece of thin foam, fabric glue, heavy cardboard, and straight pins. Trace the pattern in the Appendix onto tissue paper, then onto heavy cardboard. Cut out card-board, including center oval. Cut a piece of thin foam, thick quilt batting, or needle punch identical to the cardboard. Layer the finished needlework, foam, and cardboard face down, centering all. Pull needlework selvages taut over the cardboard and glue to the back of cardboard, holding it in place with straight pins set close together into the card-board. Let it dry. From the center of the needle-work, cut pie-shaped spokes back toward the em-broidery (not too far). Turn these back taut over the cardboard and glue as before. This will make the opening for the photo. Let it dry. Cut a second piece of cardboard without the center hole. Cover this with more of the same material and fashion a stand, if desired. Glue or stitch to the first piece of cardboard, wrong sides together. Leave one side open for inserting photographs.

Fittings

There are several kinds of fittings available for embroidered wall hangings, bellpulls, and samplers. Most are made of wrought iron or brass. Some are very simple and others more ornate. They come in many sizes, and perhaps the best way to get the correct size is to select one after the project is completed. Choose one closest in size to the embroidery. Remember if you plan to use fittings, the top (and bottom, if desired) hems must be wide enough to hold the dowel or rod and open at the ends for insertion. For a minibellpull, a brass belt ring available at any fabric store works well.

Frames

Needlework can be enhanced by a frame; with framing as with storing, however, needlework needs to breathe. Moisture trapped under glass can cause rotting and mildew. Glass also flattens the stitching unless held away from it by matting. Finally, glass may distort colors and make the needlework more difficult to see. I find this especially true of nonglare glass, which also contains chemicals that may be harmful to needlework in the long run. I suggest framing needlework without glass. If you desire a soft look, a piece of foam can be placed behind the embroidery. An occasional vacuuming will keep most such needlework clean. If you wish to use glass, however, make sure the framing is not airtight so the needlework can still breathe and see that the glass is held away from the threads by mattes or spacers.

Chapter Six
Patterns and Instructions

Given in this chapter are the instructions for each of the fifty-eight designs in this book. As in Chapter Four they are organized in collections, beginning with The Homestead Collection and ending with The Folklore Collection.

At the beginning of each set of instructions I list the technique and materials used to make the sample shown in the color photographs, then I suggest alternate thread materials that can be used on the same fabric, and finally the size of fabric needed to make the sample, in that order. Finally there are instructions for beginning the design, regardless of the materials in which it is worked.

Each design has a color chart and a graphic pattern. The color chart lists at least two sets of colors: one for the thread or yarn used in the sample and one in an alternative thread or yarn.

When working in wool on canvas, remember that the entire piece must be filled in, whereas on fabric, the cloth itself can be left open and incorporated into the design. With many of the color keys, the fill-in colors for canvas are listed at the bottom. The abbreviations in the color keys are as follows:

DMC = DMC embroidery floss
DFT = Danish Flower Thread
KL = Kulört or Klippans linen thread
LW = Laine separable wool by DMC
AW = Anchor tapisserie wool
GW = Guro wool-synthetic blend tapestry yarn
Cross-stitch = Cross-stitch or any of the other three counted thread stitches (refer to sample instructions for stitch used in colorplate)

Most of the designs can be worked in several mediums, not all of which are listed with the instructions. Review the information in Chapter Five and charts 3, 4, and 5 in the Appendix for ideas on changing materials. Chapter Five also includes instructions on finishing projects.

The Homestead Collection

Most of the samples made for the designs in The Homestead Collection are worked in cross-stitch. The colors are traditional Norwegian steel blue, orange-red, and mustard-yellow except in The Lord's Prayer Sampler, which uses shades of dusty rose (also an old favorite in Scandinavia) and mauve with the blue. For all of these I used DMC floss, from 2 to 6 strands.

The Homestead Table Runner and Bellpull are worked on 11-count aida. The runner is 12 inches wide, the bellpull is 4 inches x 20 inches. The Gudbrandsdal Dolls are worked on a 15-count linaida cloth. The woman is 9 inches tall, the man 10 inches tall, and the sheep 4 inches x 6 inches in size. The pillows and baskets are made of 15-count linaida as well. Of the three picture designs—farm couple, sheep, and chickens—each can be made into pillows, baskets, wall pictures, or other items. In the samples the farm couple is made into a pillow of orange-red wool, while the sheep picture is a pillow of teal blue corduroy. The chickens picture is used here on a basket lined and covered with red cotton.

Most of the pieces in this collection can be worked on any size counted thread fabric. The Rosemaling Snapshot Frames and the Sheep Jumper for little girls, however, must be worked on fabric that holds 14 stitches to the inch in order to come out the correct size. Because the frames are made using just four shades of any one color, it is quite simple to change colors to match any decor or taste. In the instructions with the graphics I have suggested several possible color schemes. The jumper in the sample is sewn of natural muslin, while the dress underneath is in gray-blue linen-look fabric. It is a Simplicity pattern. These sheep and hearts can also be embroidered on a small boy's romper if it has a rectangular yoke or bib or on any fabric using waste canvas, even sweat shirts and sweaters. Waste canvas is available at needlework and fabric stores.

If you are a beginner looking for a first project, or if you would like to make a quick gift, the breadcloth can be made in a day. The breadcloth,
napkins, and place mats are all made of salem cloth, which can be bought precut, hemmed, and fringed for table settings in many needlework stores. Salem, a synthetic, is ideal for embroidered pieces that will require repeated washings. The bibs and tray liner can be made quickly. The bibs can be special baby gifts. The samples are worked on scraps of salem and aida fabrics, both of which are washable. The wooden trays can be purchased in Scandinavian gift shops. They come in many sizes, and the tray liner can be made larger or smaller to fit any size.

The Homestead Collection Samplers—the Norseman Sampler, the Lord's Prayer Sampler, and the Baby's Room Sampler—are all worked on 26-count bleached linen in the samples. Because of the small verse worked over only one thread, the Norseman Sampler must be worked on linen-weave fabrics. However, the others may be worked on cotton aida cloth or any of the many synthetic counted thread fabrics or on colored or natural linen. I have included color charts for stitching them in Danish Flower Thread as well as DMC embroidery floss.

THE NORSEMAN SAMPLER *(COLORPLATE 1)*

Technique: Cross-stitch.
Materials: Linen, 26 count bleached.
DMC embroidery floss, use 2 strands.
Danish Flower Thread, use 1 strand.
Cut size: 20 inches x 26 inches.
Finished size: 14 inches x 20 inches.

One square on the pattern equals 2 threads on linen weaves. This piece must be worked on linen weave because the inset poem is worked over one thread. Be careful not to pull the threads too tight. Find the center of the pattern with the aid of the arrows. Find the center of the cloth. Begin here. When stitching is completed fill in the entire border with DMC #927 or DFT #229, both light blue. For stitches and finishing see Chapter Five. Compose the initials and date for the sampler with the aid of the alphabet provided in the Appendix. Use your own initials as the signature or, for a wedding or anniversary, the initials of the couple and the date in the middle.

French knot	backstitch	cross-stitch	DMC	DFT
		• • / • •	927	229
		OO / OO	926	227
•	⌐	●● / ●●	924	228
		ω ω / ω ω	761	12
		\\ / \\	3328	96
		XX / XX	349	500
		= = / = =	902	14
	⌐	■	3371	240
		★★ / ★★	725	48
	V	△△ / △△	3347	40
		▲▲ / ▲▲	320	10
		↔↔ / ↔↔	645	19
		∴∴ / ∴∴	948	28
		↑↑ / ↑↑	712	0

top

Among the rocks by t
The Norseman a ho
There with his wife &
He sows life and

The Norseman Sampler ***(upper left)***

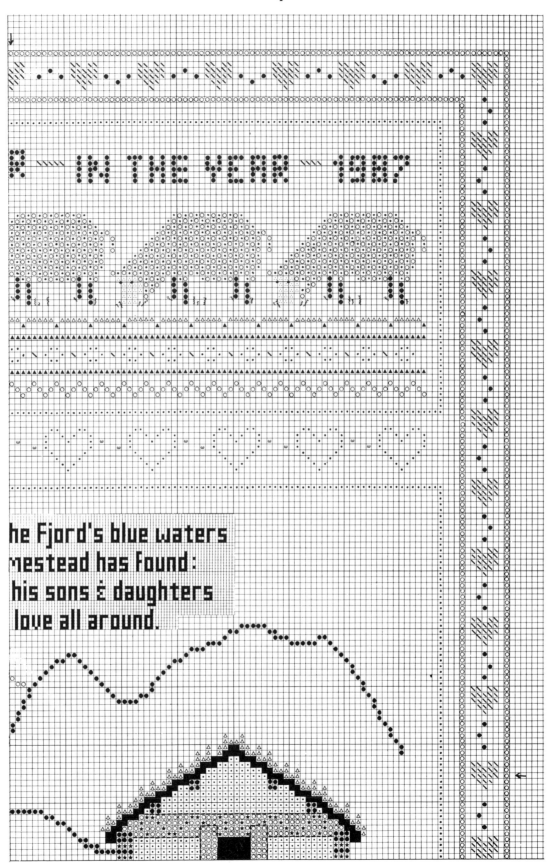

The Norseman Sampler *(upper right)*

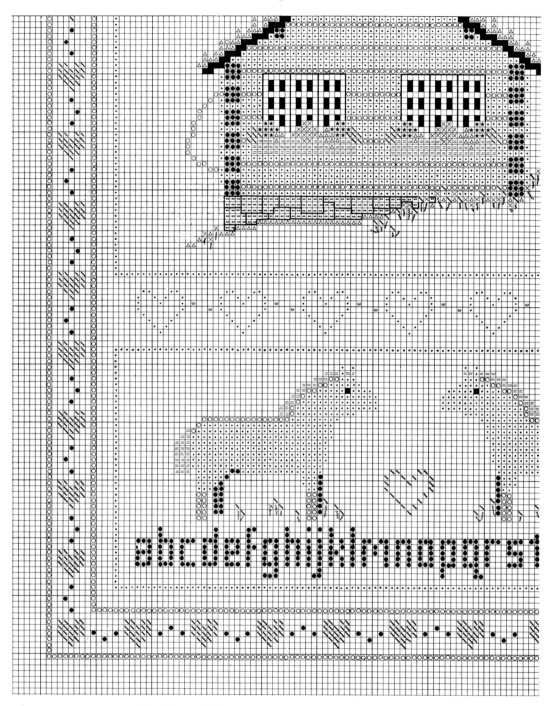

The Norseman Sampler *(lower left)*

The Norseman Sampler *(lower right)*

HOMESTEAD PICTURES—SHEEP, CHICKENS, AND FARM COUPLE *(COLORPLATE 2)*

Technique: Cross-stitch.
Materials: Linaida, 15 count tweed gray-brown.
DMC embroidery floss, use 2 strands.
Danish Flower Thread, use 1 strand.
Cut sizes: Sheep 10 inches x 10 inches; chickens 10 inches x 8 inches; farm couple 9 inches x 9 inches.
Finished sizes: Sheep 6 inches x 6 inches; chickens 6 inches x 4 inches; farm couple 5 inches x 5 inches.

One square on the pattern equals 1 square on aida weaves and 2 threads on linen weaves and canvas. Find the center of the pattern with the aid of the arrows. Find the center of the cloth. Begin here. For stitches and finishing see Chapter Five. To use wool on canvas see Chapter Five.

Sheep

	DMC	AW
	927	158
	926	162
	924	164
	902	341
	320	215
	3347	266
	948	194
	3371	987

Chickens

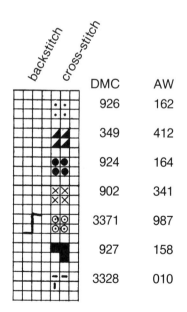

	DMC	AW
	926	162
	349	412
	924	164
	902	341
	3371	987
	927	158
	3328	010

Farm Couple

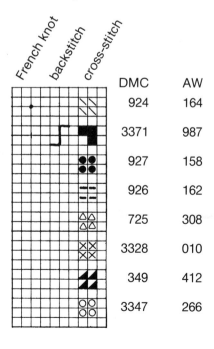

	DMC	AW
	924	164
	3371	987
	927	158
	926	162
	725	308
	3328	010
	349	412
	3347	266

top

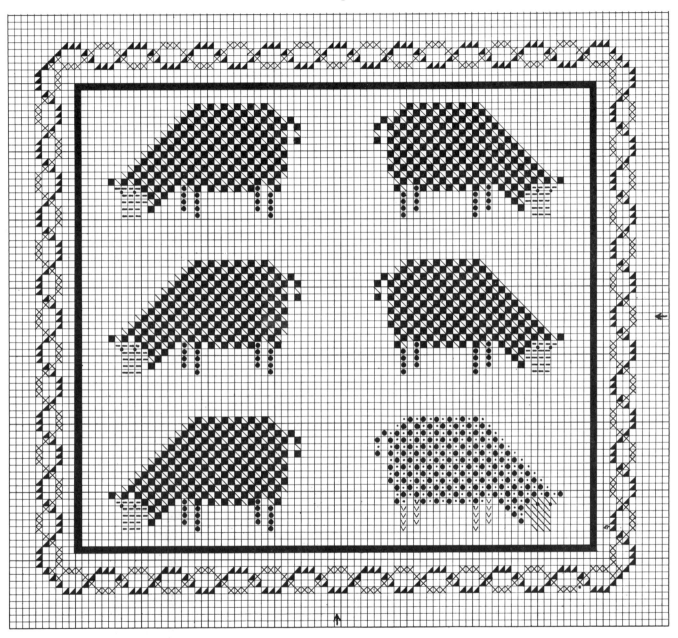

Homestead Pictures—Sheep

top

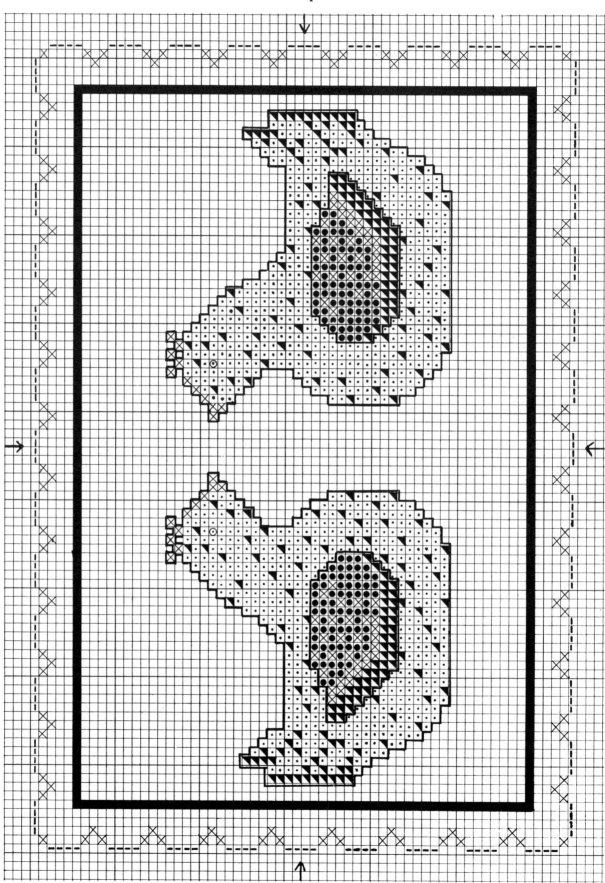

Homestead Pictures—Chickens

top

Homestead Pictures—Farm Couple

GUDBRANDSDAL DOLLS *(COLORPLATE 2)*

Technique:	Cross-stitch.
Materials:	Linaida, 15 count tweed gray-brown.
	DMC, use 2 strands for little stitches, 6 strands for large stitches.
Cut sizes:	Woman 10 inches x 16 inches; man 10 inches x 16 inches; sheep 10 inches x 8 inches.
Finished sizes:	Woman 4 inches x 10 inches; man 4 inches x 10 inches; sheep 6 inches x 4 inches.

One square on the pattern equals 1 square on aida weaves and 2 threads on linen weaves. Note that the large stitches take up 4 squares. Find the center of the pattern with the aid of the arrows. Find the center of the cloth. Begin here. For stitches and finishing see Chapter Five. To use wool on canvas or separable wool on even-weave fabric see Chapter Five.

Sheep

backstitch cross-stitch

		DMC	AW
	✕	926	849
	◼	3371	987

Man

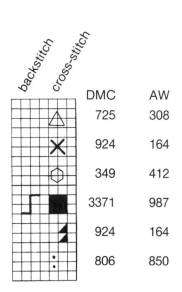

backstitch cross-stitch

		DMC	AW
	△	725	308
	✕	924	164
	⬡	349	412
	◼	3371	987
	◢	924	164
	⋮	806	850

Woman

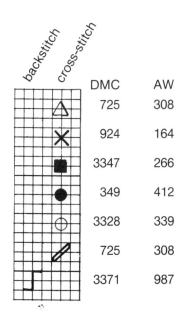

backstitch cross-stitch

		DMC	AW
	△	725	308
	✕	924	164
	◼	3347	266
	●	349	412
	⊕	3328	339
	◿	725	308
		3371	987

top

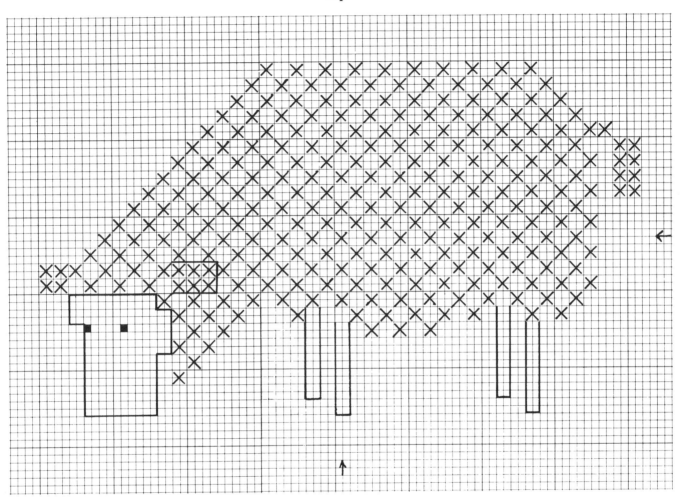

Gudbrandsdal Dolls—Sheep

top

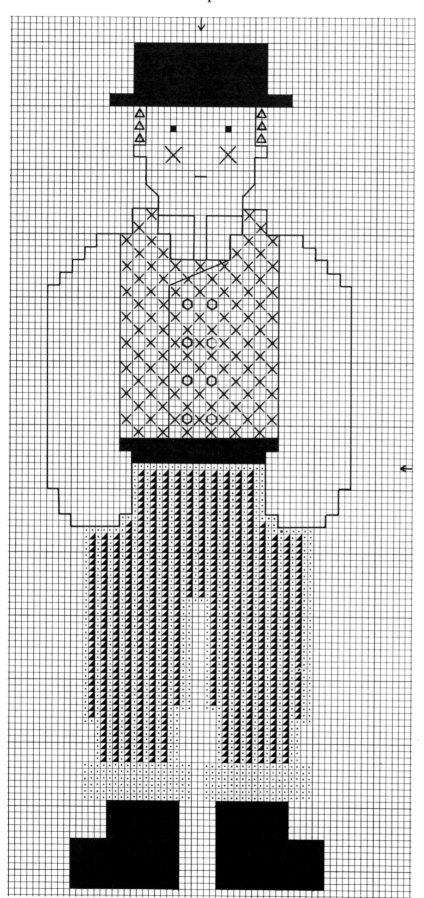

Gudbrandsdal Dolls—Man

top

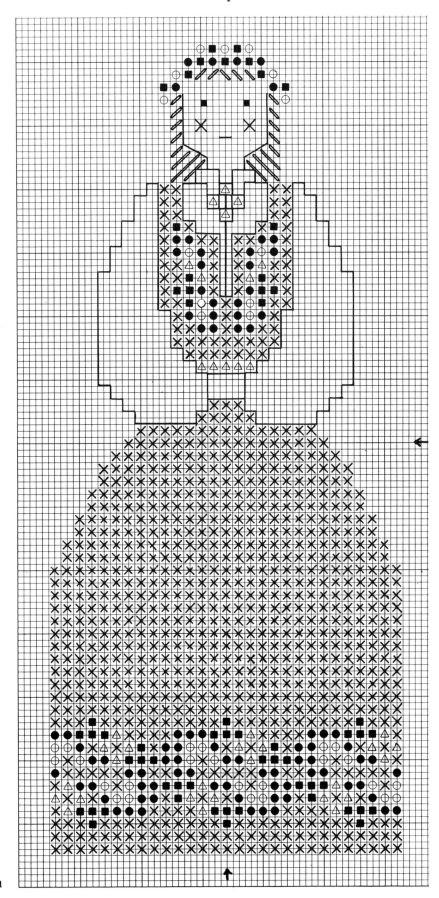

Gudbrandsdal Dolls—Woman

HOMESTEAD SHEEP—BREADCLOTH, NAPKIN, AND PLACE MAT *(COLORPLATE 2)*

Technique: Cross-stitch.
Materials: Salem cloth, 26 count ecru.
DMC embroidery floss, use 2 strands.
Danish Flower Thread, use 1 strand.
Finished sizes: Large breadcloth 18 inches x 18 inches; small breadcloth 16 inches x 16 inches; large napkin 14 inches x 14 inches; small napkin 12 inches x 12 inches; place mat 18½ inches x 13 inches.

One square on the pattern equals 2 threads on linen weaves and 1 square on aida weaves. Prepare cloth according to instructions on page 59 or buy ready-made. Begin stitching 8 threads (4 squares) up from the bottom of cloth, in the center on place mats, and in the corner on breadcloths and napkins. For stitches and finishing see Chapter Five. If planning to hemstitch edges cut all pieces 1½ inches wider and 1½ inches longer.

Breadcloth and Napkin

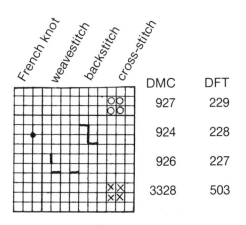

				DMC	DFT
French knot	weavestitch	backstitch	cross-stitch	927	229
				924	228
				926	227
				3328	503

Place Mat

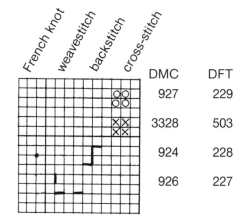

				DMC	DFT
French knot	weavestitch	backstitch	cross-stitch	927	229
				3328	503
				924	228
				926	227

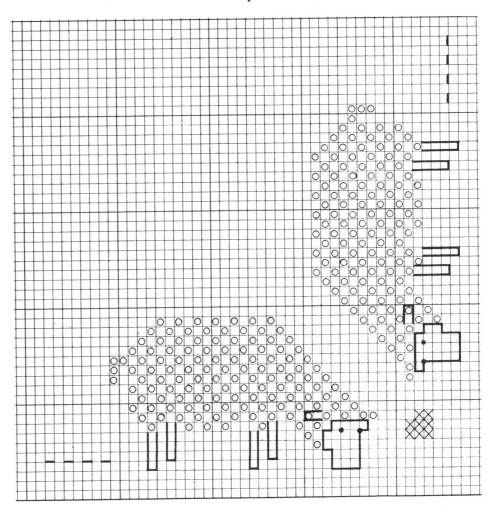

Homestead Sheep—Breadcloth and Napkin

top

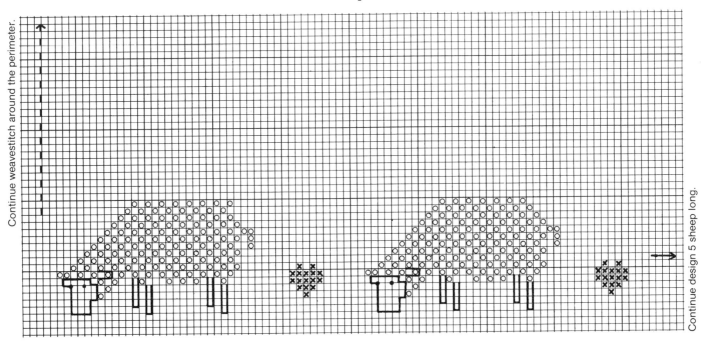

Homestead Sheep—Place Mat

HEARTS TRAY LINER *(COLORPLATE 2)*

Technique: Cross-stitch.
Materials: Salem, 26 count ecru.
DMC embroidery floss, use 2 strands.
Danish Flower Thread, use 1 strand.
Cut size: 8 inches x 8 inches.
Finished size: 6 inches x 6 inches.

This border design can be adapted to any size tray by repeating the hearts to achieve the desired length. It also may be used for place mats, napkins, table runners, or skirt borders.

One square on the pattern equals 2 threads on linen weaves and 1 square on aida weaves. Begin by stitching the outside row of the pattern, starting 1 inch up from the edges in a corner. When the pattern is completed cut away selvage to 6 threads from stitching and fringe. For stitches and finishing see Chapter Five.

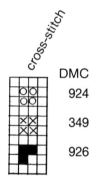

cross-stitch	DMC
⊙⊙	924
✕✕	349
■	926

top

Hearts Tray Liner

THE LORD'S PRAYER SAMPLER
(COLORPLATE 3)

		DMC	DFT
Technique:	Cross-stitch.		
Materials:	Linen, 26 count bleached.		
	DMC embroidery floss, use 2 strands.		
	Danish Flower Thread, use 1 strand.		
Cut size:	20 inches x 27 inches.		
Finished size:	14 inches x 21 inches.		

One square on the pattern equals 2 threads on linen weaves and 1 square on aida weaves. Find the center of the pattern with the aid of the arrows. Find the center of the cloth. Begin here. For stitches and finishing see Chapter Five. Compose the name and date for the sampler with the aid of the alphabet provided in the Appendix.

backstitch	cross-stitch	DMC	DFT
	• • / • •	316	3
	x x / x x	3041	27
	△△ / △△	315	4
	Y Y / Y Y	3046	225
	○ ○ / ○	927	229
	╱╱ / ╱╱	926	227
	★★ / ★★	924	228
	◥ ◣	646	302
	∂ ∂ / ∂ ∂	451	19
	◢◣	3052	223
	■	413	32

top

The Lord's Prayer Sampler *(upper left)*

The Lord's Prayer Sampler *(upper right)*

The Lord's Prayer Sampler *(lower left)*

The Lord's Prayer Sampler *(lower right)*

ROSEMALING SNAPSHOT FRAMES
(COLORPLATE 7)

cross-stitch		DMC	DMC	DMC	DMC
■	dark	902	336	935	3031
△△	medium dark	335	517	3346	829
●●	medium light	899	518	470	831
✕✕	light	3326	519	471	834
		pink	**blue**	**green**	**brown**

Technique: Cross-stitch.
Materials: Aida, 14 count ecru.
DMC embroidery floss, use 2 strands.
Danish Flower Thread, use 1 strand.
Cut size: 11 inches x 13 inches.
Finished size: 5 inches x 7 inches.

One square on the pattern equals 1 square on aida weaves and 2 threads on linen weaves. (Material must hold 13 to 14 stitches per inch.) Find the center bottom of the pattern with the aid of the arrows. Begin 1½ inches up on the bottom of the aida, centering (short side). For stitches and finishing see Chapter Five.

top

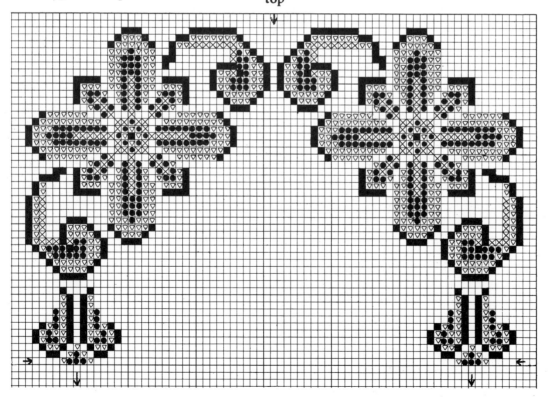

Rosemaling Snapshot Frames

Plate 1

The Norseman Sampler

Plate 2

Homestead Pictures—Farm Couple,
Chickens, and Sheep

Gudbrandsdal Dolls

Homestead Sheep—Breadcloth,
Place Mat, and Napkin; Hearts
Tray Liner

Plate 3

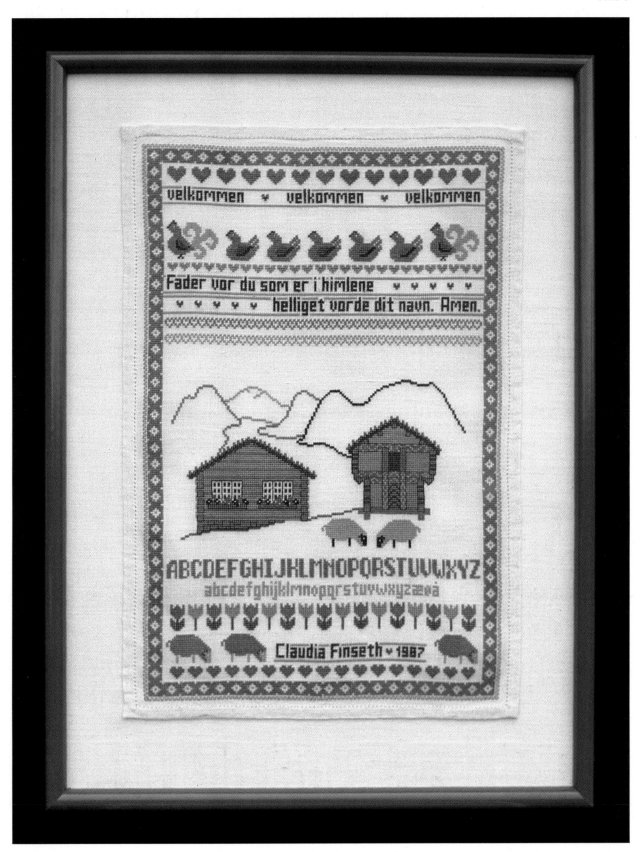

The Lord's Prayer Sampler

Plate 4

Baby's Room Sampler

Plate 5

Sheep Bib

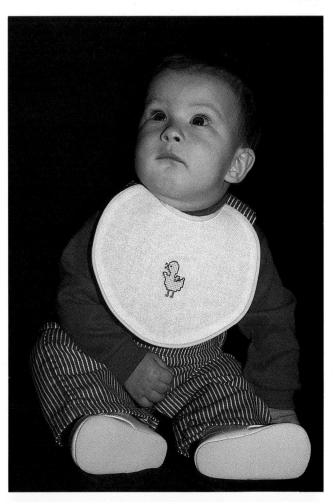

Chick Bib

Little Girl's Sheep Jumper

Plate 6

Homestead Table Runner

Homestead Bellpull—Sample 1

Plate 7

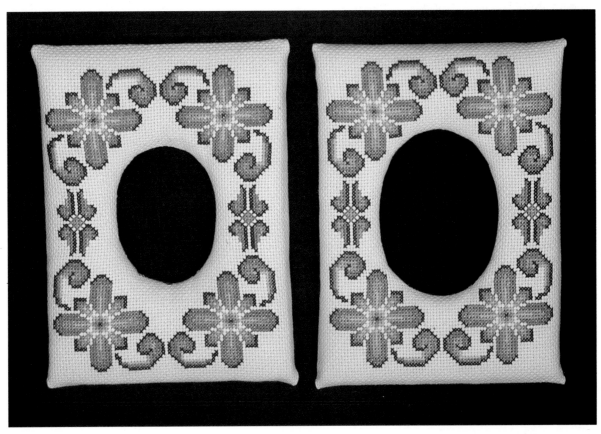

Rosemaling Snapshot Frames

Snowflake Table Runner

Plate 8

Snowflake Bellpull—Sample 2

Plate 9

Snowflake Picture—Sample 1

Snowflake Picture—Sample 2

Snowflake Picture—Sample 3

Plate 10

Snowflake—Breadcloth, Place Mat, and Napkin; Snowflake Tray Liner

Gift Bag

Snowflake Tree Decorations

Plate 11

Little Girl's Reindeer
Jumper

Reindeer Bib

Plate 12

Reindeer Stocking

Plate 13

St. Lucia Stocking

Plate 14

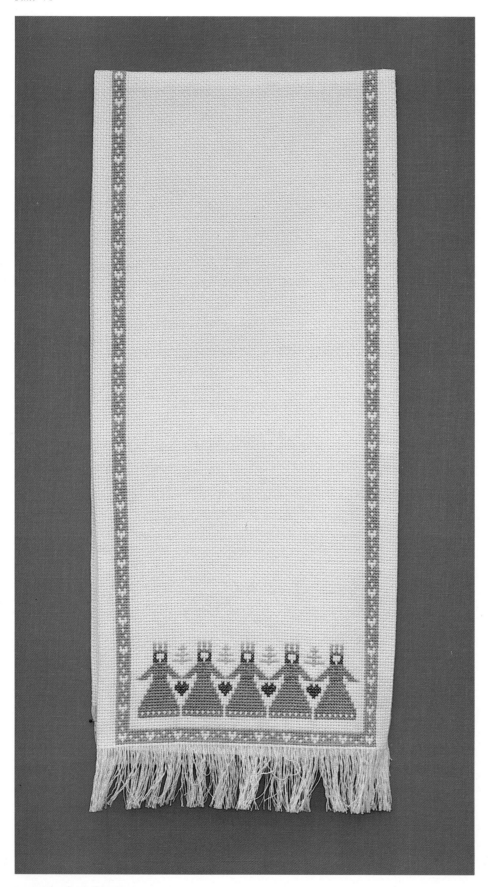

Lucia Bride Table Runner

Plate 15

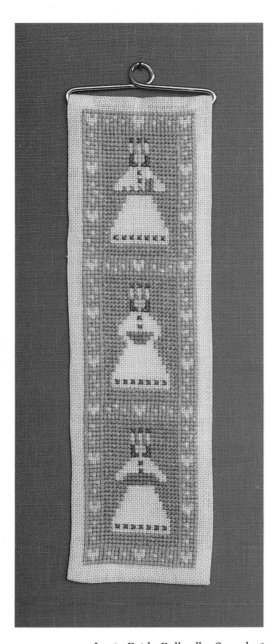

Lucia Bride Bellpull—Sample 1

Lucia Bride Bellpull—Sample 2

Plate 16

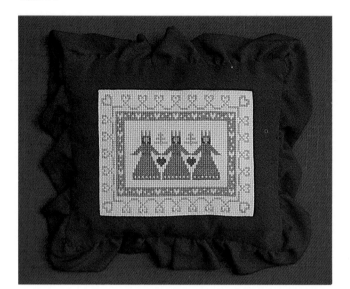

Lucia Bride Picture

Bethlehem Scene (blue)—Sample 1

Bethlehem Scene (rose)—Sample 2

Bethlehem Scene (lavender)—Sample 3

Plate 17

Danish Dolls in Hedebo Costume

Icelandic Doll

Plate 18

Finnish Dolls in Karelian Costume

Norwegian Dolls in Hardanger
Costume

Plate 19

Swedish Woman in Hälsingland Costume (above and below), Swedish Doll in Dalarna Costume, and Swedish Man in Hälsingland Costume

Plate 20

Lapp Dolls in Finmark Costume

Fafnismol Wall Hanging

Plate 21

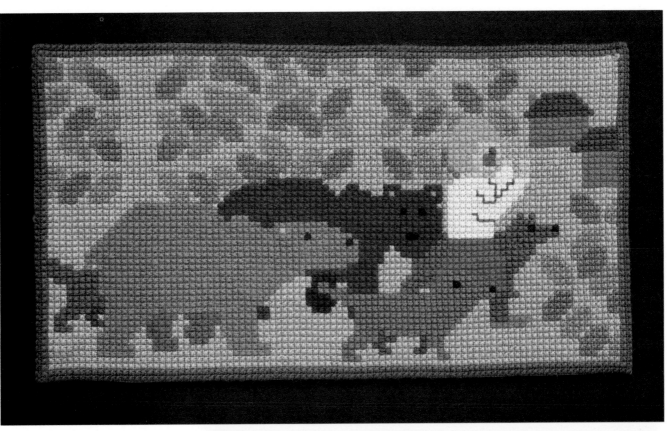

Kalevala Wall Hanging—
Sample 1

Kalevala Wall Hanging—Sample 2

Plate 22

The Snow Queen Wall Hanging

East o' the Sun and West o' the Moon Wall Hanging—
Sample 1

East o' the Sun and West o' the Moon Wall
Hanging—Sample 2

Plate 23

The Wonderful Adventures of Nils Wall Hanging

Plate 24

Lapp Magic Drum Symbol—Reindeer 1

Lapp Magic Drum Symbol—Reindeer 3

Lapp Magic Drum Symbol—Reindeer 2

BABY'S ROOM SAMPLER *(COLORPLATE 4)*

Technique:	Cross-stitch.
Materials:	Linen, 26 count bleached.
	DMC embroidery floss, use 2 strands.
	Danish Flower Thread, use 1 strand.
Cut size:	16 inches x 19 inches.
Finished size:	10 inches x 13 inches.

One square on the pattern equals 2 threads on linen weaves and 1 square on aida weaves. Find the center of the linen. Begin here. When stitching is completed fill in the entire border with DMC #927 or DFT #21, both light blue.

DMC	DFT
924	228
926	27
927	21
347	503
3328	235
902	411
725	203
744	31
948	25
3371	240

Baby's Room Sampler *(upper half)*

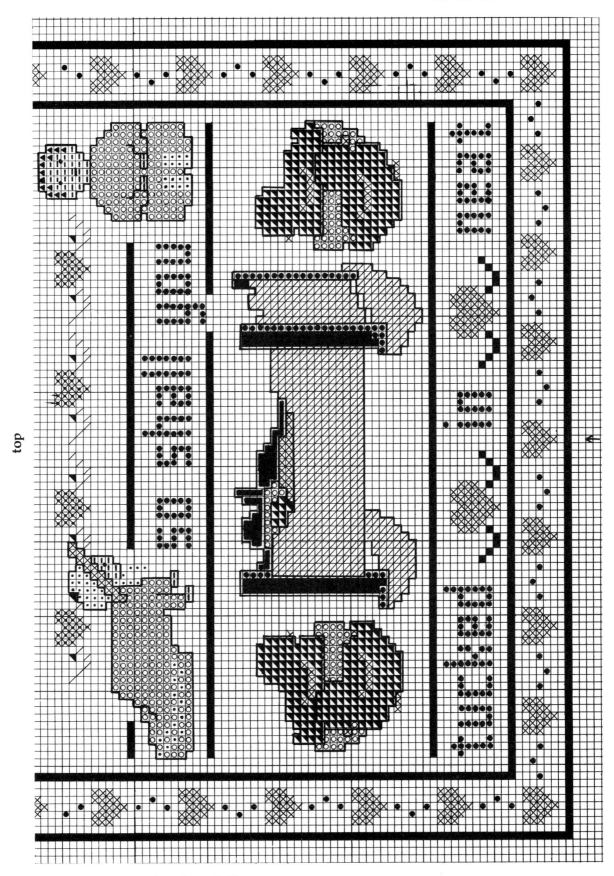

top

Baby's Room Sampler *(lower half)*

SHEEP BIB AND CHICK BIB *(COLORPLATE 5)*

Chick

			DMC	DFT
French knot	backstitch	cross-stitch		
		╱╱	744	31
		♥♥ ♥♥	3328	503
•	⌐		3371	216

Technique:	Cross-stitch.
Materials:	Salem, 14 count ecru and 26 count white.
	DMC embroidery floss, use 2 strands.
	Danish Flower Thread, use 1 strand.
Cut sizes:	10 inches x 10 inches, each.
Finished sizes:	7 inches x 7 inches, each.

Sheep

			DMC	DFT
French knot	backstitch	cross-stitch		
		◉◉ ◉◉	760	2
		╲╲	927	229
•	⌐		924	220

One square on the pattern equals 2 threads on linen weaves and 1 square on aida weaves. Trace the pattern from the Appendix onto tissue paper. Cut out bib and zigzag edges. Center the design 2½ inches from the bottom edge of the bib. For stitches and finishing see Chapter Five.

top

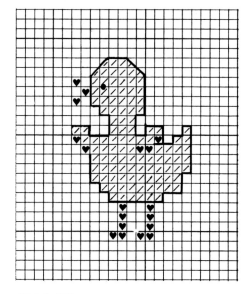

Chick Bib

top

Sheep Bib

LITTLE GIRL'S SHEEP JUMPER
(COLORPLATE 5)

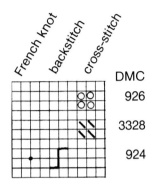

Technique: Cross-stitch.
Materials: Aida, 14 count ecru.
DMC embroidery floss, use 2
strands.
Danish Flower Thread, use 1
strand.
For yoke, use any Simplicity
pattern or any straight-yoked
jumper pattern, adjusting the
design to fit accordingly.
(Zigzag the edges of the yoke.)

One square on the pattern equals 1 square on
aida weaves and 2 threads on linen weaves.
(Material must hold 13 to 14 stitches per inch.)
Find the center of the pattern with the aid of the
arrows. Find the center of the yoke. Begin here.
For stitches and finishing see Chapter Five.

top

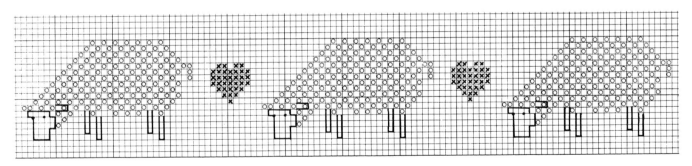

Little Girl's Sheep Jumper

HOMESTEAD TABLE RUNNER
(COLORPLATE 6)

		backstitch	cross-stitch	DMC	AW
			■	926	162
			●● ●●	924	164
			✕✕ ✕✕	347	412
			▨▨	902	341
			△△ △△	725	308
			▨▨ ▨▨	3371	987
			○○ ○○	3052	266

Technique: Cross-stitch.
Materials: Aida, 11 count ecru.
                    DMC embroidery floss, use 3
                       strands.
Cut size: 15 inches x any length.
Finished size: 11 inches x any length.

    One square on the pattern equals 1 square on aida weaves and 2 threads on linen weaves. Find the center bottom of the pattern with the aid of the arrows. Find the center of one end of the cloth. Begin here, about 30 squares up from the edge. For stitches and finishing see Chapter Five. To use wool on canvas or separable wool on even-weave wool fabric see Chapter Five.

Homestead Table Runner *(bottom)*

HOMESTEAD BELLPULL *(COLORPLATE 6)*

Technique: Sample 1, cross-stitch.
Materials: Aida, 11 count ecru.
DMC embroidery floss, use 3 strands.
Danish Flower Thread, use 2 strands.
Cut size: 8 inches x 21 inches.
Finished size: 4 inches x 17 inches.

Technique: Sample 2, cross-stitch.
Materials: Even-weave wool, 18 count khaki and Laine wool.
Laine separable wool, use 1 strand.
Cut size: 25 inches x 8 inches.
Finished size: 21 inches x 4 inches.

One square on the pattern equals 1 square on aida weaves and 2 threads on linen weaves and canvas. Find the center of the pattern with the aid of the arrows. Find the center of the cloth. Begin here. For stitches and finishing see Chapter Five. To use wool on canvas see Chapter Five.

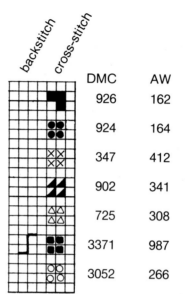

		DMC	AW
		926	162
		924	164
		347	412
		902	341
		725	308
		3371	987
		3052	266

backstitch   cross-stitch

top   top

bottom   bottom

Homestead Bellpull *(upper half)*   **Homestead Bellpull** *(lower half)*

The Snowflake Collection

The Snowflake Collection is a group of monochromatic designs, that is, they call for only one color of floss or yarn and a contrasting background fabric. Most of the sample pieces are worked with white DMC floss on navy blue aida fabric. They could just as well be embroidered in any color of thread on white cloth, or conversely in white or ecru floss on any color of counted thread fabric—brown, red, green, or light blue, for example. Colors can be chosen to accent or match a particular decor. The designs in The Snowflake Collection may also be worked in wools on canvas or even-weave wool using *gobelin*, double cross-stitch, or long-armed cross-stitch as well as cross-stitch.

If you would like to make a gift but are short on time, or if you are a beginner looking for a first project, the breadcloths and the bookmark or minibellpull make up very quickly. The samples of the breadcloth, napkin, place mat, and tray liner are worked on synthetic salem cloth for easy washing. The wooden tray can be purchased at Scandinavian gift shops. The bookmark is worked on Ribband, which has prefinished edges. The tree decorations are small, fast projects and are a good way to use up scraps of cloth and floss. The Reindeer Bib can be made of larger scraps for a baby gift. The little Gift Bag is another quick project and can be filled with a tiny surprise and hung on the Christmas tree.

The Reindeer Jumper is the only design in this collection that must be embroidered on a certain size counted thread fabric—13 or 14 stitches per inch. It is a Simplicity pattern for sizes 3 to 6. The sample jumper is embroidered on navy aida cloth sewn to a very light, soft navy linen-look fabric. The dress underneath (also in the Simplicity pattern) is of white cotton shirting.

The Snowflake Table Runner is on 14-count aida and is 14 inches wide. It works nicely not only on a dinner table, but on a buffet or coffee table as well. Somehow mine always ends up on my old oak, standing wall cupboard, where it fits perfectly. The Snowflake Bellpull can double as another smaller table runner or be hung on the wall. The three Snowflake Pictures are versatile; they can be made into pillows, baskets, or wall pictures. The two made into sample pillows are embroidered on navy aida, and the pillows are sewn of soft navy flannel wool accented with white cotton lace.

Some color suggestions for The Snowflake Collection are: DMC embroidery floss #817 (red), #911 (green), or #823 (blue) on white cloth; Danish Flower Thread #88 (red), #234 (violet), or #230 (periwinkle) on white; DMC ecru on brown aida. The Reindeer Jumper can be embroidered in red or green on white aida and sewn of white cotton fabric, and the dress can be made of red or green material to match the embroidery.

SNOWFLAKE TABLE RUNNER
(COLORPLATE 7)

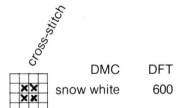

	DMC	DFT
snow white		600

Technique: Cross-stitch.
Materials: Aida, 14 count navy.
                    DMC embroidery floss, use 2
                        strands.
                    Danish Flower Thread, use 1
                        strand.
Cut size: 19 inches x any length desired.
Finished size: 15 inches x any length desired.

One square on the pattern equals 1 square on aida weaves and 2 threads on linen weaves. Find the center bottom of the pattern with the aid of the arrows. Find the center of one end of the cloth. Begin here, about 30 squares up from the edge. For stitches and finishing see Chapter Five. To use wool on canvas see Chapter Five.

top

Snowflake Table Runner *(lower left)*

Snowflake Table Runner *(lower right)*

SNOWFLAKE BELLPULL *(COLORPLATE 8)*

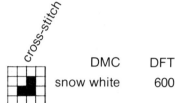

	DMC	DFT
	snow white	600

Technique: Sample 1, cross-stitch.
Materials: Aida, 14 count navy.
                    DMC embroidery floss, use 2
                       strands.
Cut size: 7 inches x 17 inches.
Finished size: 3 inches x 13 inches.

One square on the pattern equals 1 square on the aida and 2 threads on linen.

Technique: Sample 2, cross-stitch.
Materials: Aida, 14 count navy.
                    DMC embroidery floss, use 4
                       strands.
Cut size: 14 inches x 34 inches.
Finished size: 8 inches x 28 inches.

One square on the pattern equals 4 squares on the aida. Find the center of the pattern with the aid of the arrows. Find the center of the cloth. Begin here. For stitches and finishing see Chapter Five. To use wool on canvas see Chapter Five.

Snowflake Bellpull *(upper half)*

Snowflake Bellpull *(lower half)*

SNOWFLAKE PICTURES *(COLORPLATE 9)*

Technique: Cross-stitch.
Materials: Aida, 14 count navy.
DMC embroidery floss, use 2 strands.
Danish Flower Thread, use 1 strand.
Cut sizes: 5 inches x 5 inches, each.
Finished sizes: 3 inches x 3 inches, each.

One square on the pattern equals 1 square on aida weaves and 2 threads on linen weaves and canvas. Find the center of the pattern with the aid of the arrows. Find the center of the cloth. Begin here. For stitches and finishing see Chapter Five. To use wool on canvas see Chapter Five.

These designs can be used for wall pictures, pillows, baskets, doilies, and many other articles.

Picture 1

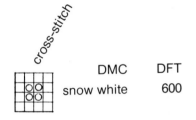

	DMC	DFT
	snow white	600

Picture 2

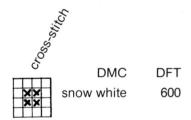

	DMC	DFT
	snow white	600

Picture 3

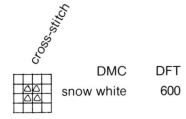

	DMC	DFT
	snow white	600

top

Snowflake Pictures—1

top

Snowflake Pictures—2

top

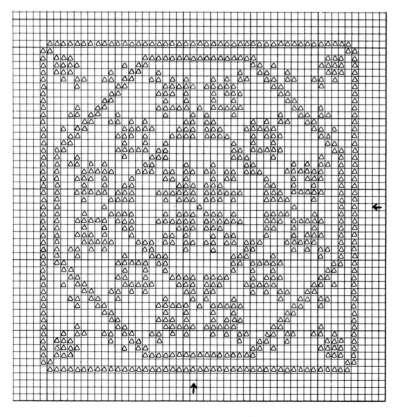

Snowflake Pictures—3

SNOWFLAKE—BREADCLOTH, NAPKIN, AND PLACE MAT *(COLORPLATE 10)*

Breadcloth and Napkin

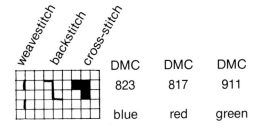

Technique: Cross-stitch.

Materials: Salem cloth, 26 count white.
DMC embroidery floss, use 2 strands.
Danish Flower Thread, use 1 strand.

Finished sizes: Large breadcloth 18 inches x 18 inches; small breadcloth 16 inches x 16 inches; large napkin 14 inches x 14 inches; small napkin 12 inches x 12 inches; place mat 18½ inches x 13 inches.

Place Mat

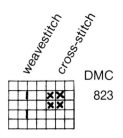

One square on the pattern equals 2 threads on linen weaves and 1 square on aida weaves. Prepare cloth according to instructions on page 59 or buy ready-made. Begin stitching 8 threads (4 squares) up from the bottom of cloth, in the center on place mats, and in the corner on breadcloths and napkins. For stitches and finishing see Chapter Five. If planning to hemstitch edges cut all pieces 1½ inches wider and 1½ inches longer.

top

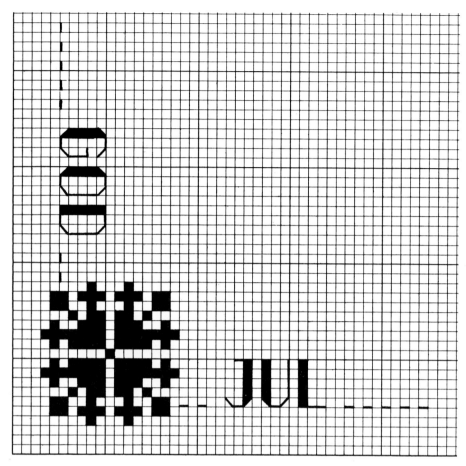

Snowflake—Breadcloth and Napkin

top

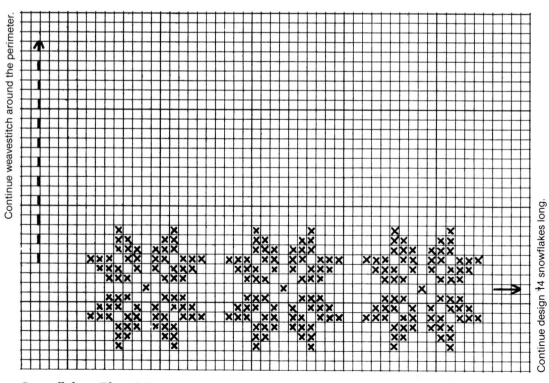

Continue weavestitch around the perimeter.

Continue design 14 snowflakes long.

Snowflake—Place Mat

SNOWFLAKE TRAY LINER *(COLORPLATE 10)*

Technique: Cross-stitch.
Materials: Salem, 26 count white.
DMC embroidery floss, use 2
    strands.
Danish Flower Thread, use 1
    strand.
Cut size: 8 inches x 8 inches.
Finished size: 6 inches x 6 inches.

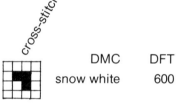

	DMC	DFT
	snow white	600

One square on the pattern equals 2 threads on linen weaves and 1 square on aida weaves. Begin by stitching the outside row of the pattern, starting 1 inch up from the edges in a corner. When the pattern is completed cut away selvage to 6 threads from stitching and fringe. For stitches and finishing see Chapter Five.

This border design can be adapted to any size tray by repeating the hearts to achieve the desired length. It may also be used for place mats, napkins, and table runners.

top

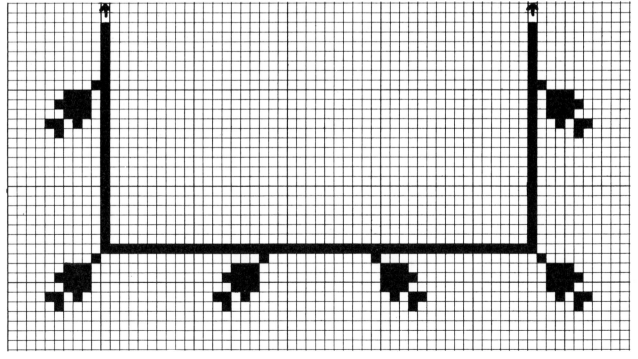

Snowflake Tray Liner

GIFT BAG *(COLORPLATE 10)*

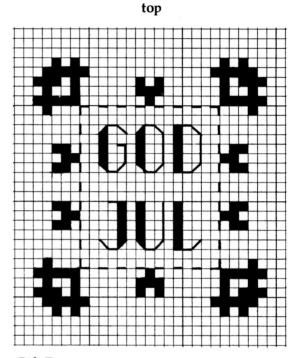

top

Gift Bag

Technique: Cross-stitch.
Materials: Salem, 26 count ecru.
DMC floss, use 2 strands.
Danish Flower Thread, use 1
strand.
Cut size: 4½ inches x 9 inches.
Finished size: 2¾ inches x 3¾ inches.

One square on the pattern equals 2 squares on the fabric. Find the center of the pattern with the aid of the arrows. Fold the fabric in half lengthwise. Find the center of the top half. Begin here. For stitches and finishing see Chapter Five.

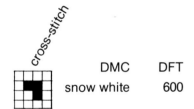

cross-stitch

	DMC	DFT
	snow white	600

SNOWFLAKE TREE DECORATIONS
(COLORPLATE 10)

cross-stitch

	DMC	DFT
snow white	600
or	or
742	48
or	or
666	500

Technique: Cross-stitch.
Materials: Scraps of salem cloth.
DMC embroidery floss, use 2 strands.
Danish Flower Thread, use 1 strand.
Cut size: 3 inches x 3 inches or larger for easy handling.
Finished size: 1 inch x 1 inch.

One square on the pattern equals 2 threads on linen weaves and 1 square on aida weaves. Find the center of the pattern with the aid of the arrows. Find the center of the cloth. Begin here. For stitches and finishing see Chapter Five.

The minibellpull or bookmark is made by running several snowflakes along a piece of Ribband, spaced about 5 squares (10 threads) apart. This is only one example of the many ways such small designs can be combined and used.

top

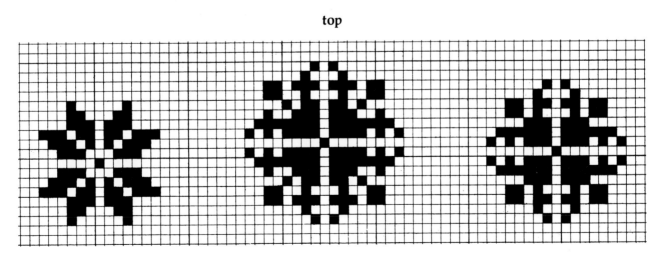

Snowflake Tree Decorations

LITTLE GIRL'S REINDEER JUMPER
(COLORPLATE 11)

Technique: Cross-stitch.
Materials: Aida, 14 count navy.
DMC embroidery floss, use 2
  strands.
Danish Flower Thread, use 1
  strand.
For yoke, use any Simplicity
  pattern or any straight-yoked
  jumper, romper, or overall
  pattern, adjusting the design
  to fit accordingly. (Zigzag the
  edges of the yoke.)

One square on the pattern equals 1 square on aida weaves and 2 threads on linen weaves. (Material must hold 13 to 14 stitches per inch.) Find the center of the pattern with the aid of the arrows. Find the center of the yoke. Begin here. For stitches and finishing see Chapter Five.

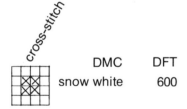

	DMC	DFT
	snow white	600

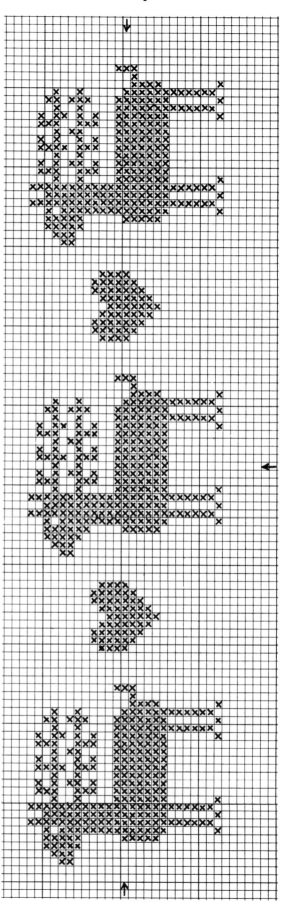

Little Girl's Reindeer Jumper

REINDEER BIB *(COLORPLATE 11)*

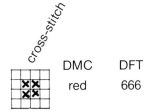

		cross-stitch	DMC	DFT
			red	666

Technique: Cross-stitch.
Materials: Salem, 26 count white.
DMC embroidery floss, use 2
   strands.
Danish Flower Thread, use 1
   strand.
Cut size: 10 inches x 10 inches.
Finished size: 7 inches x 7 inches.

One square on the pattern equals 2 threads on
linen weaves and 1 square on aida weaves. Trace
the pattern from the Appendix onto tissue paper.
Cut out bib and zigzag edges. Center the design
2½ inches from the bottom of the bib. For stitches
and finishing see Chapter Five.

top

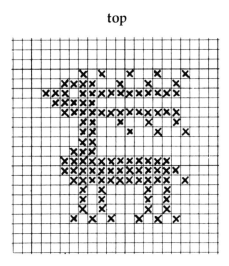

Reindeer Bib

Bits of Christmas

The samples made up for this collection vary widely; they use all four of the counted thread stitches described in this book as well as combinations of wool, floss, canvas, linen, and cotton aida cloth. All of this variety in a small collection of just six designs illustrates how many ways counted thread can be worked.

The two Christmas stocking samples are embroidered in wool using *gobelin* stitch on 14-count (7½ stitches per inch) penelope canvas. They are about 14 inches long and 7 inches wide. I backed them with wool flannel cut from an old pair of my husband's trousers and lined them with some light rayon fabric. Larger stockings can be made using a larger penelope canvas: 12 count would make stockings about 17 inches long, 10 count would make stockings about 21 inches long. For long-armed cross-stitch or double cross-stitch, use 10-count or larger canvas to be able to fit in the stitches. Smaller stockings can be made by using 30-count linen (15 stitches per inch) or 15- or 18-count aida cloth with embroidery floss or Danish Flower Thread. (For figuring sizes see chart 2 in Chapter Five.)

The sample Lucia Bride Picture—here made into a pillow with a cranberry linen-look fabric—and the Lucia Bride Table Runner are worked on 11-count ecru aida cloth embroidered in dusty rose, cranberry, and steel-blue DMC floss. The table runner is 8 inches wide. It can be made wider or narrower simply by stitching more or fewer Lucia Brides. Each figure adds about 1½ inches on 11-count aida, so 7 would make a runner 11 inches wide, while 3 would result in a 5-inch-wide runner.

There are two samples of the Lucia Bride Bellpull. The smaller is 9 inches long, worked in DMC floss on 26-count linen. This is small enough for a bookmark. The larger sample is embroidered with wool in *gobelin* stitch on 12-count penelope canvas and is about 20 inches long. In long-armed cross-stitch or double cross-stitch on 9-count penelope, it would be almost 30 inches in length.

The Bethlehem Scene is a monochromatic design using only one color when embroidered on linen, aida, or other finished cloth. I have worked one sample on bleached 30-count linen in lilac Danish Flower Thread. Because it requires just one color, it is easy to adapt to any taste or color scheme; just choose the color you desire. When worked in wools on canvas, the Bethlehem Scene requires a second color to fill in the background. The samples show it in double cross-stitch in two shades of blue and in long-armed cross-stitch in dusty rose and plum. Because of its simple color, this design especially reveals the rich textures of these two stitches.

REINDEER STOCKING AND ST. LUCIA STOCKING *(COLORPLATE 12–13)*

Technique:	*Gobelin* stitch.	
Materials:	Penelope canvas, 14 count brown.	
	Anchor yarn, use 1 strand.	
Cut size:	13 inches x 20 inches.	
Finished size:	7 inches x 14 inches.	

One square on the pattern equals 2 upright *gobelin* stitches over 2 threads. Find the center of the pattern with the aid of the arrows. Find the center of the canvas. Begin here. For stitches and finishing see Chapter Five.

These designs also may be worked in DMC embroidery floss, Danish Flower Thread, or linen thread on linen, aida, or other counted thread material; in these cases the background need not be filled in. For changing materials, stitches, and finishing see Chapter Five. For letters and numbers to change the names and dates on the stockings see the alphabet in the Appendix.

Reindeer

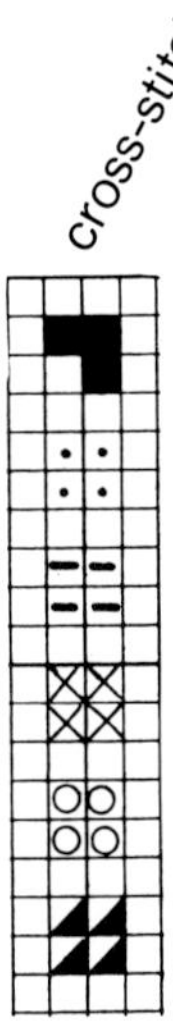

cross-stitch

	AW	DMC	DFT
	163	924	220
	860	502	9
	987	3371	240
	390		
	896	315	411
	871	3041	29

St. Lucia

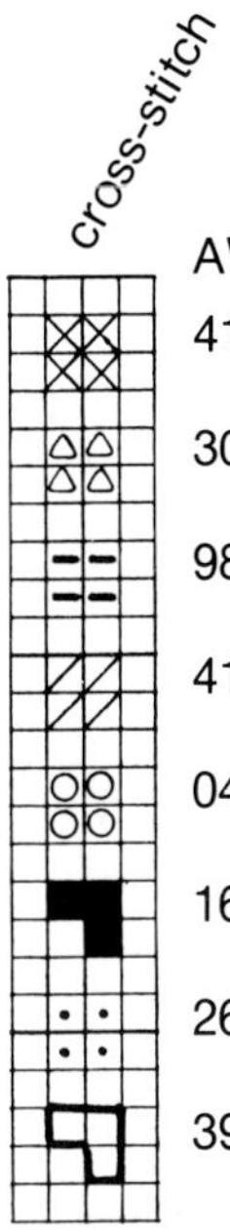

cross-stitch

	AW	DMC	DFT
	419	975	216
	308	725	54
	987	3371	240
	412	349	500
	045	902	411
	163	924	220
	266	3347	237
	390		

top

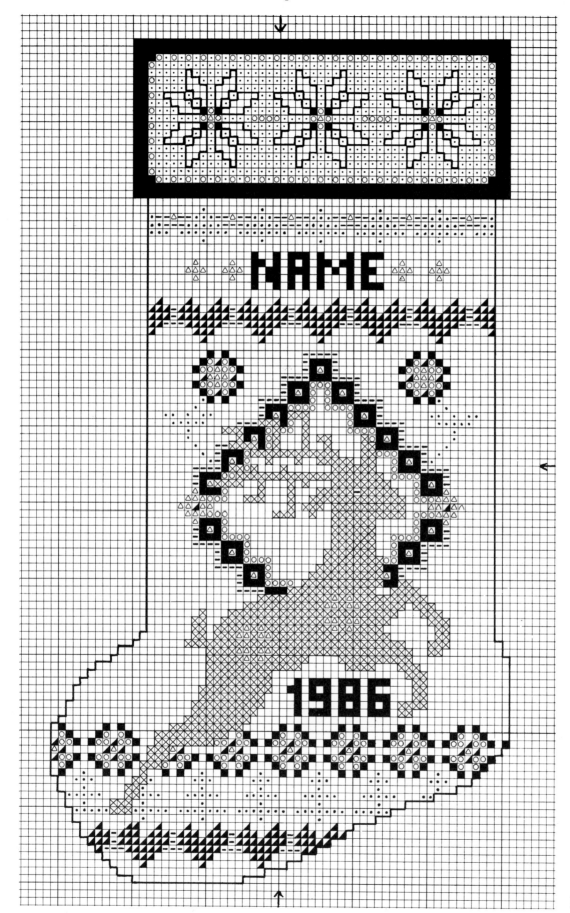

Reindeer Stocking

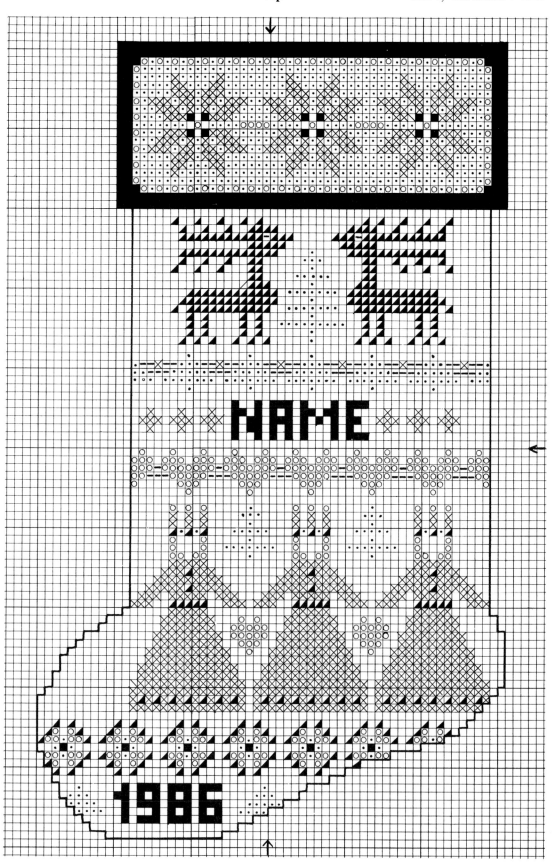

St. Lucia Stocking

LUCIA BRIDE TABLE RUNNER
(COLORPLATE 14)

	cross-stitch	DMC	AW
	■■ ■■	926	162
	+|+ +|+	927	161
	●● ●●	315	870
	△△ △△	928	158
	✕✕ ✕✕	316	067
	·· ··	778	981
fill in background			386

Technique: Cross-stitch.
Materials: Aida, 11 count ecru.
DMC embroidery floss, use 3
    strands.
Danish Flower Thread, use 2
    strands.
Cut size: 15 inches x any length.
Finished size: 9½ inches x any length.

One square on the pattern equals 1 square on aida weaves and 2 threads on linen weaves. Find the center bottom of the pattern with the aid of the arrows. Find the center of one end of the cloth. Begin here, about 30 squares up from the edge. For stitches and finishing see Chapter Five. To use wool on canvas or separable wool on even-weave fabric see Chapter Five.

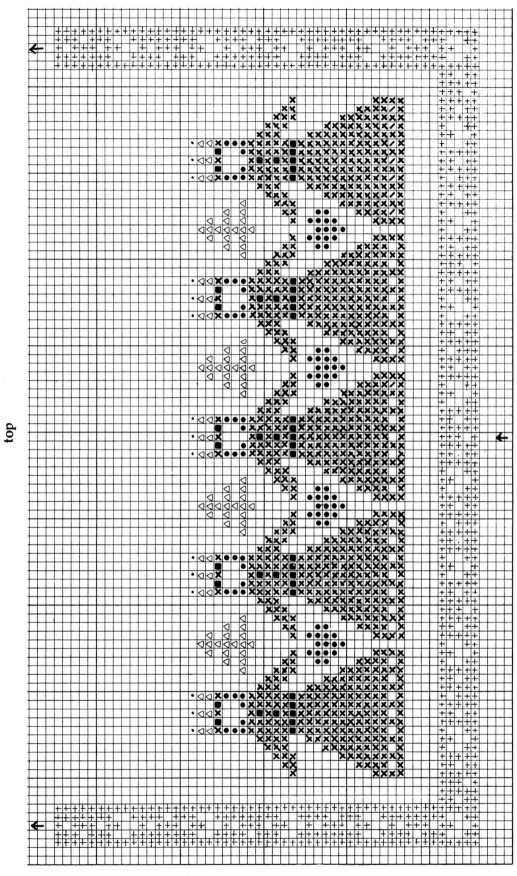

top

Lucia Bride Table Runner

LUCIA BRIDE BELLPULL (COLORPLATE 15)

Technique:	Sample 1, cross-stitch.
Materials:	Linen, 26 count bleached.
	DMC embroidery floss, use 2 strands.
	Danish Flower Thread, use 1 strand.
Cut size:	6 inches x 14 inches.
Finished size:	3 inches x 9½ inches.

Technique:	Sample 2, *gobelin* stitch.
Materials:	Penelope canvas, 12 count brown.
	Anchor wool, use 1 strand.
Cut size:	9 inches x 24 inches.
Finished size:	5 inches x 20 inches.

One square on the pattern equals 2 upright *gobelin* stitches over 2 threads or one cross-stitch. Find the center of the pattern with the aid of the arrows. Find the center of the canvas. Begin here. For stitches and finishing see Chapter Five. To make a larger bellpull work 3 upright *gobelin* stitches over 3 threads for each square on the pattern or work long-armed cross-stitch or double cross-stitch on larger count canvas.

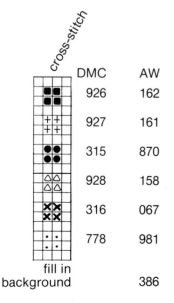

	DMC	AW
■■	926	162
++	927	161
●●	315	870
△△	928	158
✕✕	316	067
··	778	981
fill in background		386

Lucia Bride Bellpull

LUCIA BRIDE PICTURE *(COLORPLATE 16)*

Technique: Cross-stitch.
Materials: Aida, 11 count ecru.
DMC embroidery floss, use 3 strands.
Danish Flower Thread, use 2 strands.
Cut size: 14 inches x 12 inches.
Finished size: 8 inches x 6 inches.

One square on the pattern equals 1 square on aida weaves and 2 threads on linen weaves. Find the center of the pattern with the aid of the arrows. Find the center of the cloth. Begin here. For stitches and finishing see Chapter Five.

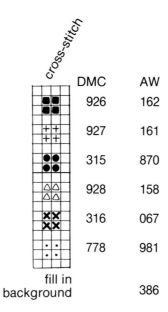

	DMC	AW
cross-stitch		
■■ / ■■	926	162
++ / ++	927	161
●● / ●●	315	870
△△ / △△	928	158
✕✕ / ✕✕	316	067
· · / · ·	778	981
fill in background		386

top

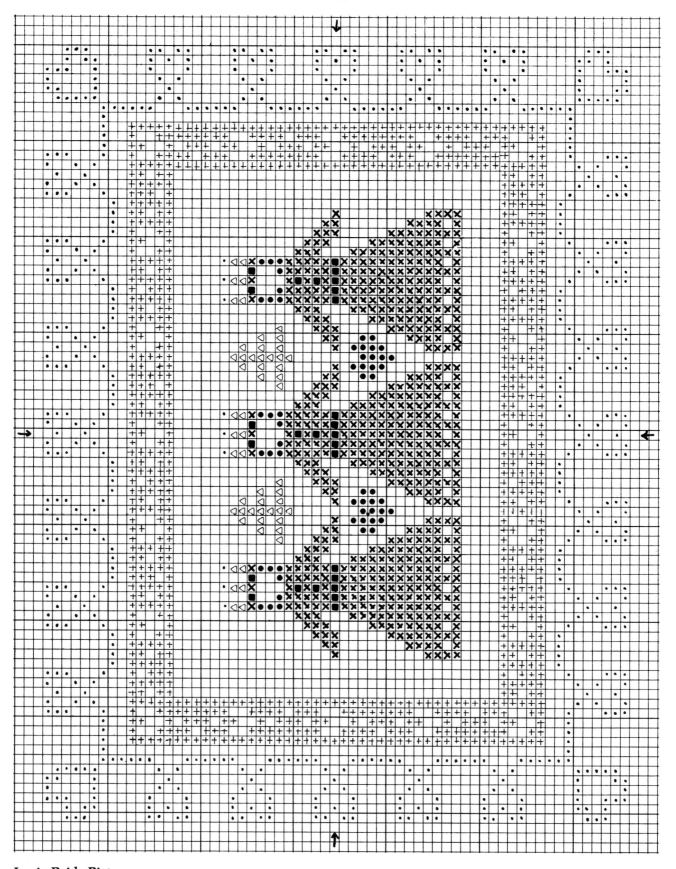

Lucia Bride Picture

BETHLEHEM SCENE *(COLORPLATE 16)*

		cross-stitch	DFT	AW	AW
	XX		233	851	430
	XX				
fill in				848	869
				blue	**rose**

Technique: Sample 1, double cross-stitch.
Materials: Penelope canvas, 9 count brown.
                  Anchor wool, use 1 strand.
Cut size: 18 inches x 22 inches.
Finished size: 14 inches x 18 inches.

Technique: Sample 2, long-armed cross-stitch.
Materials: Penelope canvas, 9 count brown.
                  Anchor wool, use 1 strand.
Cut size: 18 inches x 22 inches.
Finished size: 14 inches x 18 inches.

Technique: Sample 3, cross-stitch.
Materials: Linen, 30 count bleached.
                  DMC embroidery floss, use 2
                      strands.
                  Danish Flower Thread, use 1
                      strand.
Cut size: 8 inches x 9 inches.
Finished size: 4 inches x 5 inches.

One square on the pattern equals 2 double threads on canvas, 1 square on aida weaves, and 2 threads on linen weaves. Find the center of the pattern with the aid of the arrows. Find the center of the canvas or cloth. Begin here. For stitches and finishing see Chapter Five.

When worked on fine linen this design can even be used for very special Christmas cards.

top

Bethlehem Scene

The Folk Costume Collection

Most of the examples of the designs for The Folk Costume Collection are stitched in DMC embroidery floss using 2 strands on fabrics with 13 to 15 stitches per inch. The Danish Dolls are stitched using 1 strand of Danish Flower Thread. About half of the figures are embroidered in cross-stitch, the other half in long-armed cross-stitch.

I designed these figures as primitive dolls. They vary somewhat in height, from 7 inches to 10 inches tall as worked in the samples. I wanted them to be a nice size for a little girl or boy to hold or arrange on her or his bed or to set in a basket by the hearth or on a table. They could even be hung on a Christmas tree. The designs also work quite well framed. If you would like a costumed couple together in one frame, just stitch them a few threads apart on the same piece of fabric with the bottoms of their feet on the same thread. Larger dolls can be made using larger count materials. A conversion chart is included in Chapter Five, The Folk Costume Collection, Dimensions for Dolls.

I suggest you choose the fabric for these dolls according to your preferences and the way in which the dolls will be used. If they are to be a child's toy, you may wish to use washable fabric, such as aida or salem cloth, or a darker fabric such as natural or "dirty" linen. If they are for decoration, any fabric is suitable. I find the heaviness of salem cloth or aida make nice smooth shapes when stuffed as dolls. Larger dolls can be made using canvas and wool or separable wool on even-weave wool cloth (see Chapter Five).

On these doll patterns the areas of clothing that should be white, such as blouses, shirts, aprons, shawls, stockings, and women's cap brims, have been left blank and are denoted by a dashed line. On white fabric it is not necessary to fill in these white areas; instead, simply follow the dashed lines, outlining them in gray. On colored fabrics, fill these areas in with white and use gray backstitching only to separate one white area from another, such as a sleeve from an apron or a collar from the shirt front. Consult the color plates of the dolls for help in identifying the white areas on each figure.

Areas that should be flesh tone have also been left blank in these patterns, but outlined in a solid line to differentiate them from the white areas. These flesh areas are the faces and hands of the dolls. Again, whether they are filled in or left unstitched will depend on the color of the background fabric. Generally it is not necessary on ecru, light brown, or natural colors. On these simply outline flesh areas with black. On white or colored fabrics, I suggest you use DMC #951 or #738 or Danish Flower Thread #25 or #28 in a simple cross-stitch for faces and hands, and the cheek and hair stitching worked over them. When the flesh areas are stitched in, use backstitching only to separate chin from neck and ears from face, but do not outline the entire face. A good rule for outlining is to do only as much as is essential to the design and no more, otherwise the work tends to take on a cartoonish look.

For some figures, three-quarter stitches have been used occasionally to depict a diagonal angle. These are made by stitching one stroke the full length and the other only a half length, making sure it goes over the first stroke to tack it down.

The strands of hair are made using 4 to 6 strands of DMC or 2 strands of DFT, one long stitch for each strand. Rosy cheeks may be depicted with one large cross using double the usual number of strands or a regular-size cross for each square on the graph. What looks best will vary with materials used, so experiment a bit.

DANISH DOLLS IN HEDEBO COSTUME
(COLORPLATE 17)

Technique: Cross-stitch.
Materials: Linen, 26 count natural.
DMC embroidery floss, use 2 strands.
Danish Flower Thread, use 1 strand.
Cut sizes: 10 inches x 16 inches, each.
Finished sizes: 4 inches x 10 inches, each.

One square on the pattern equals 2 threads on linen weaves and 1 square on aida weaves. Find the center of the pattern with the aid of the arrows. Find the center of the cloth. Begin here. For stitches and finishing see Chapter Five. Be sure to read general comments on dolls at the beginning of this section.

Danish Woman

backstitch	cross-stitch	DFT	DMC
	XX	500	817
	XX	97	321
	∂∂	32	317
	ωω	19	318
	⊙⊙	211	500
	★★	508	912
	△△	86	309
	==	224	503
	••	240	310
	YY	47	833
	╲╲	510	518
	X	303	962
	╱	47	833

Danish Man

backstitch	cross-stitch	DFT	DMC
	XX	500	817
	♥♥	14	221
	★★	508	912
	••	240	310
	ωω	19	318
	++	25	437
	╲╲	510	518
	X	503	962
	□□	216	3031
	YY	47	833
		507	702
		47	833

top   **top**

Fill in entire coat with red and stitch green accents over the red.

Danish Dolls in Hedebo Costume—Woman   **Danish Dolls in Hedebo Costume—Man**

ICELANDIC DOLL *(COLORPLATE 17)*

Technique: Long-armed cross-stitch.
Materials: Salem, 14 count ecru.
DMC embroidery floss, use 2
strands.
Danish Flower Thread, use 1
strand.
Cut size: 10 inches x 15 inches.
Finished size: 4 inches x 9 inches.

One square on the pattern equals 2 threads on linen weaves and 1 square on aida weaves. Find the center of the pattern with the aid of the arrows. Find the center of the cloth. Begin here. For stitches and finishing see Chapter Five. Be sure to read general comments on dolls at the beginning of this section.

	backstitch	cross-stitch	DMC	DFT
		• • / • •	310	240
		Y Y / Y Y	742	48
	✕	● ● / ● ●	729	203
		∴ ∴ / ∴ ∴	436	250
		▫▫ / ▫▫	400	214
		▲▲ / ▲▲	921	95
		↑↑ / ↑↑	469	273
		★★ / ★★	700	508
		✕	3328	503
			414	19
			921	95

top

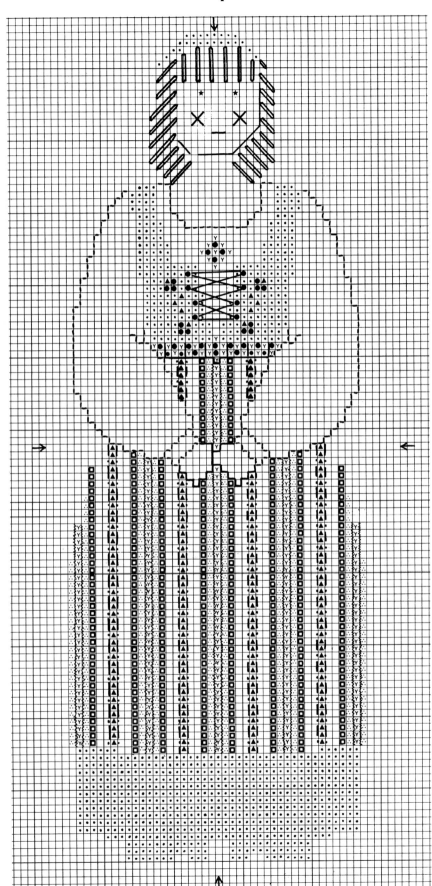

Icelandic Doll

FINNISH DOLLS IN KARELIAN COSTUME
(COLORPLATE 18)

Technique: Cross-stitch.
Materials: Linen, 26 count natural.
DMC embroidery floss, use 2 strands.
Danish Flower Thread, use 1 strand.
Cut sizes: 10 inches x 16 inches, each.
Finished sizes: 4 inches x 10 inches, each.

One square on the pattern equals 2 threads on linen weaves and 1 square on aida weaves. Find the center of the pattern with the aid of the arrows. Find the center of the cloth. Begin here. For stitches and finishing see Chapter Five. Be sure to read general comments on dolls at the beginning of this section.

Woman

backstitch	cross-stitch	DMC	DFT
		825	228
		349	500
		977	54
		414	35
		973	123
		918	213
		white	600
		3328	503
		310	240
		3021	216

Man

backstitch	cross-stitch	DMC	DFT
		437	16
		349	500
		825	228
		310	240
		977	54
		938	251
		434	213
		white	600
		3328	503
		414	35
		3021	216

top

top

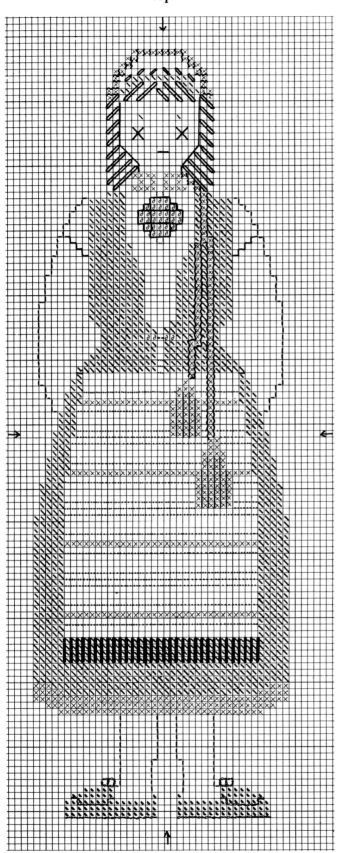

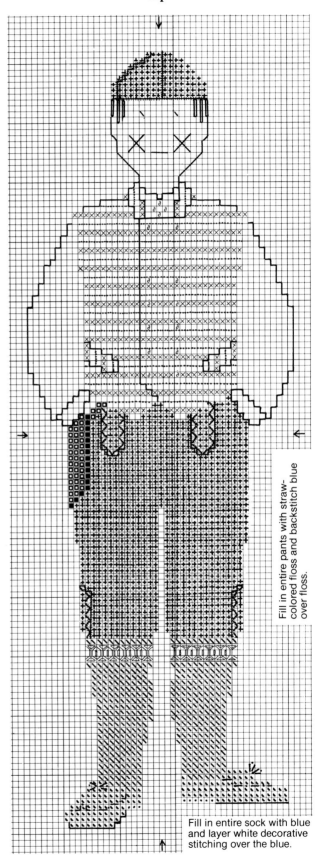

Fill in entire pants with straw-colored floss and backstitch blue over floss.

Fill in entire sock with blue and layer white decorative stitching over the blue.

Finnish Dolls in Karelian Costume—Woman

Finnish Dolls in Karelian Costume—Man

NORWEGIAN DOLLS IN HARDANGER COSTUME *(COLORPLATE 18)*

Technique:	Cross-stitch.
Materials:	Linaida, 15 count tweed gray-brown.
	DMC embroidery floss, use 2 strands.
	Danish Flower Thread, use 1 strand.
Cut sizes:	10 inches x 16 inches, each.
Finished sizes:	4 inches x 10 inches, each.

One square on the pattern equals 2 threads on linen weaves and 1 square on aida weaves. Find the center of the pattern with the aid of the arrows. Find the center of the cloth. Begin here. For stitches and finishing see Chapter Five. Be sure to read general comments on dolls at the beginning of this section.

Woman

DMC	DFT
310	240
349	500
729	203
725	48
911	8
3347	40
951	28
414	32
3328	503
924	228
610	251

Man

DMC	DFT
310	240
349	500
911	8
725	48
927	35
951	28
3328	503
414	32
924	228
610	251

top   **top**

Norwegian Dolls in Hardanger Costume—Woman   **Norwegian Dolls in Hardanger Costume—Man**

SWEDISH DOLLS IN HÄLSINGLAND
COSTUME *(COLORPLATE 19)*

Technique:	Long-armed cross-stitch.
Materials:	Salem, 26 count white.
	DMC embroidery floss, use 2 strands.
	Danish Flower Thread, use 1 strand.
Cut sizes:	10 inches x 16 inches, each.
Finished sizes:	4 inches x 10 inches, each.

One square on the pattern equals 2 threads on linen weaves and 1 square on aida weaves. Find the center of the pattern with the aid of the arrows. Find the center of the cloth. Begin here. For stitches and finishing see Chapter Five. Be sure to read general comments on dolls at the beginning of this section.

Woman

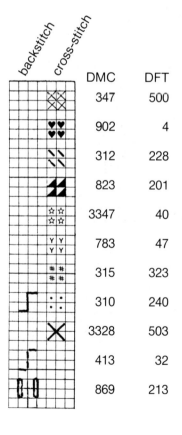

	DMC	DFT
	347	500
	902	4
	312	228
	823	201
	3347	40
	783	47
	315	323
	310	240
	3328	503
	413	32
	869	213

Man

	DMC	DFT
	310	240
	349	97
	823	201
	311	220
	725	48
	434	213
	3328	503

top

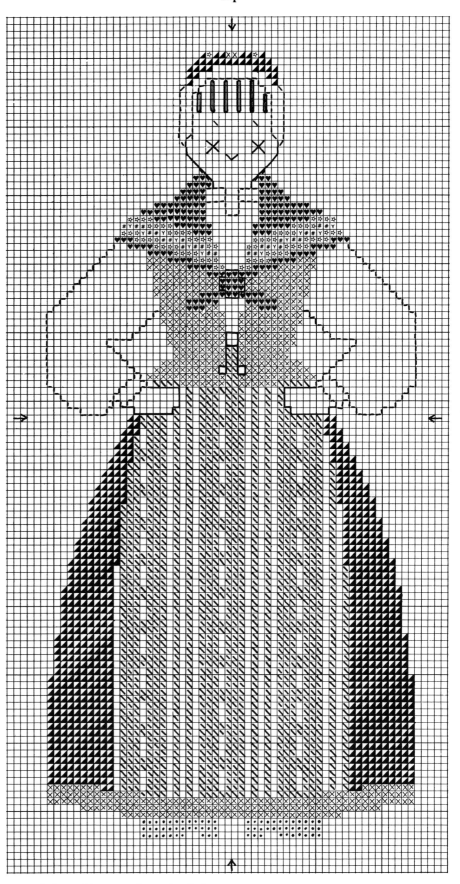

Swedish Dolls in Hälsingland Costume—Woman

top

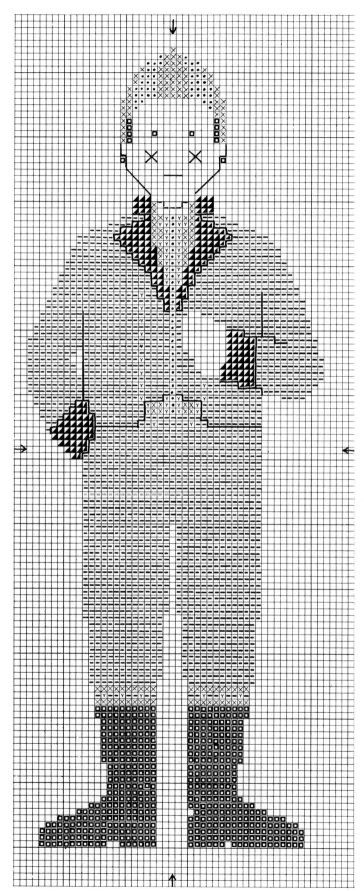

Swedish Dolls in Hälsingland Costume—Man

SWEDISH DOLL IN DALARNA COSTUME
(COLORPLATE 19)

Technique: Long-armed cross-stitch.
Materials: Salem, 26 count white.
DMC embroidery floss, use 2
    strands.
Danish Flower Thread, use 1
    strand.
Cut size: 9 inches x 14 inches.
Finished size: 3 inches x 8 inches.

One square on the pattern equals 2 threads on linen weaves and 1 square on aida weaves. Find the center of the pattern with the aid of the arrows. Find the center of the cloth. Begin here. For stitches and finishing see Chapter Five. Be sure to read general comments on dolls at the beginning of this section.

top

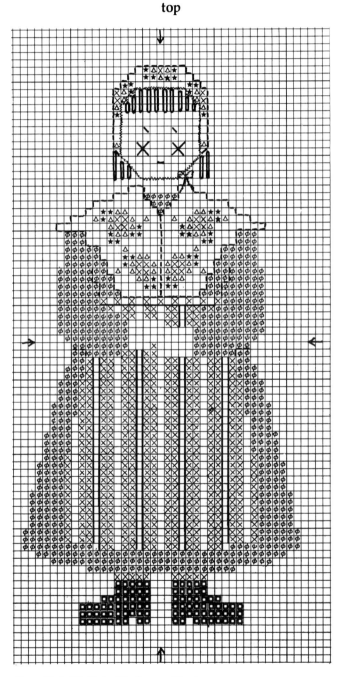

Swedish Doll in Dalarna Costume

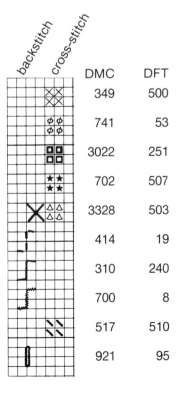

		DMC	DFT
	XX	349	500
	φφ	741	53
	□□	3022	251
	★★	702	507
X	△△	3328	503
		414	19
		310	240
		700	8
	＼＼	517	510
		921	95

LAPP DOLLS IN FINMARK COSTUME
(COLORPLATE 20)

Technique: Cross-stitch.
Materials: Linaida, 15 count ecru.
DMC embroidery floss, use 2
strands.
Danish Flower Thread, use 1
strand.
Cut sizes: Woman 10 inches x 16 inches; boy
7½ inches x 10 inches.
Finished sizes: Woman 4 inches x 10 inches; boy
3½ inches x 6 inches.

One square on the pattern equals 1 square on the aida weaves and 2 threads on linen weaves. Find the center of the pattern with the aid of the arrows. Find the center of the cloth. Begin here. For stitches and finishing see Chapter Five. Be sure to read general comments on dolls at the beginning of this section.

Woman

	backstitch / cross-stitch	DMC	DFT
	o o	995	17
	X X	666	500
⌐	◪◪	823	202
	Y Y	444	123
	★ ★	702	507
	ω ω	415	303
	✦ ✦	646	32
	▢ ▢	434	213
	X	3328	503
⌐		535	32
◿		white	600
⁄		434	213

Boy

	backstitch / cross-stitch	DMC	DFT
	▼▼	996	510
⌐	o o	995	17
	X X	666	500
	◪◪	823	202
	★ ★	702	507
	Y Y	444	123
	ω ω	415	303
	∂ ∂	646	32
	∴ ∴	3031	222
	◇ ◇	644	218
	⁄ ⁄	738	28
	φ φ	721	53
	▢ ▢	434	213
	X	3328	503
⌐		535	32

top

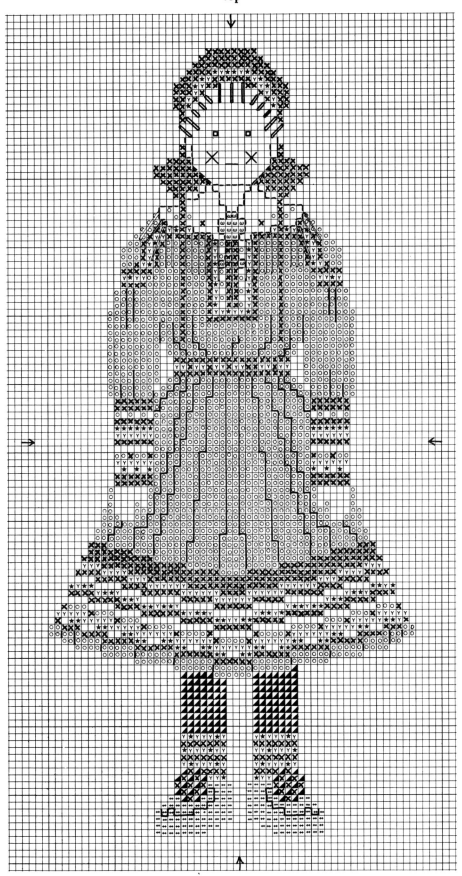

Lapp Dolls in Finmark Costume—Woman

top

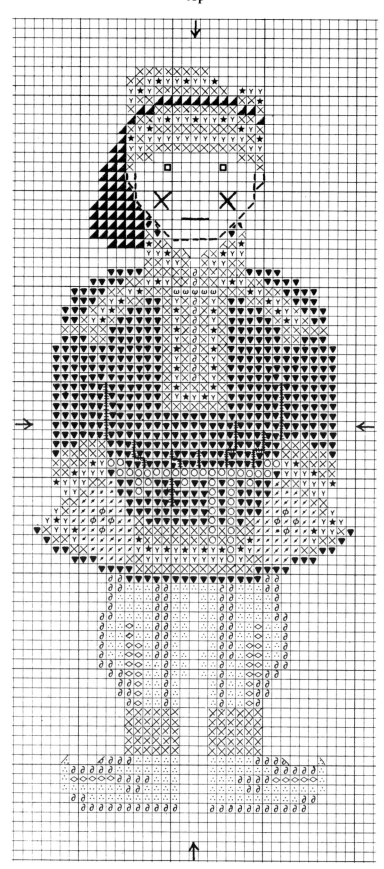

Lapp Dolls in Finmark Costume—Boy

The Folklore Collection

I originally intended the designs for The Folklore Collection to be wall hangings. I wanted them to be fairly substantial in size. So most of the samples are worked in wool on canvas in the bigger stitches, long-armed cross-stitch, and double cross-stitch. However, they also can be worked in embroidery floss or Danish Flower Thread on linen or aida for a totally different effect, very delicate and dreamlike.

The Danish, Norwegian, and Swedish tales are designed to be used individually or as a set. They might even be combined on one long canvas or piece of linen as a frieze. The wools are muted tones of sage, mauve-brown, gray-blue, and rose. The samples on canvas are worked in long-armed cross-stitch on 10-count penelope canvas and are about 16 inches x 20 inches in size. They would also be splendid in double cross-stitch or *gobelin* stitch.

The Norwegian tale, "East o' the Sun and West o' the Moon," also has been embroidered in cross-stitch using Danish Flower Thread on bleached linen. The bear and any other white areas have not been stitched but rather retain the open linen. Only the features have been outline stitched. With Danish Flower Thread it is possible to keep the colors muted and soft. This sample measures about 6 inches x 8 inches on 26-count linen. To make a frieze of all three tales—Danish, Norwegian, and Swedish—on linen, simply leave a space of 4 to 8 threads between each scene. I suggest placing the bear in the middle, the reindeer to the left, and the goose to the right in a frieze.

There are two samples of the Finnish tale. One is embroidered in wool on 9-count penelope canvas using double cross-stitch. It is approximately 11 inches x 20 inches in size. The other sample is stitched with DMC floss on 11-count ecru aida cloth and is only 4 inches x 7 inches. In both samples the colors are gray-browns, grays, silver-greens, and rusts.

The Icelandic tale is the largest of all my designs, measuring 130 stitches tall by 299 stitches wide. On 10-count penelope canvas it is 2 feet tall by 4½ feet wide. Yet stitched in Danish Flower Thread or DMC floss on 30-count linen (15 stitches per inch) it would only be 9 inches x 20 inches. The sample is worked in Guro yarn in traditional Scandinavian blues, reds, and golds with lots of tan also. Guro yarn has an attractive tweedy look to it, but it can be difficult to obtain, so I have also included a color key for Anchor wools, which are more readily available.

The Lapp Magic Drum Symbol designs use only one color. Because they are monochromatic, they could be worked in any color on white or natural fabric, or in white thread on a red, dark blue, green, or brown background. I have worked the samples in red Kulört linen thread in long-armed cross-stitch on 18-count bleached linen and in caramel and teal Danish Flower Thread in cross-stitch on 26-count bleached linen. Here are some color and material suggestions for The Lapp Magic Drum Symbol:

DMC embroidery floss #817 red, #806 turquoise, #924 steel blue, or #918 rust on bleached or natural linen; Kulört lingarn #273 gray-brown, #298 teal, or #299 cinnamon on coarse linen; Anchor wools #412 red with #332 orange background, or #987 brown-black with #392 grey-tan background.

With all of these designs a background color is needed for working in wools on canvas, while on counted thread fabric, areas can be left open and the fabric itself made a part of the design.

KALEVALA WALL HANGING *(COLORPLATE 21)*

Technique: Sample 1, double cross-stitch.
Materials: Penelope canvas, 9 count brown.
Anchor wool, use 1 strand.
Cut size: 26 inches x 17 inches.
Finished size: 20 inches x 11 inches.

Technique: Sample 2, cross-stitch.
Materials: Aida, 11 count ecru.
DMC embroidery floss, use 3
strands.
Cut size: 15 inches x 11 inches.
Finished size: 9 inches x 5 inches.

    One square on the pattern equals 2 double
threads on canvas, 2 threads on linen weaves, and
1 square on aida weaves. Find the center of the
pattern with the aid of the arrows. Find the center
of the canvas or fabric. Begin here. For stitches and
finishing see Chapter Five. Here the smaller sample
has been made into a pillow.

backstitch / cross-stitch	AW	DMC
	420	838
	360	3371
	309	317
	903	612
	904	610
	403	310
	428	355
	402	white
	347	436
	188	924
	412	347
	194	948
	348	610
	350	921
	418	610
	984	452
	985	840
	837	927
	432	503
	440	3053
fill in background	376	

Kalevala Wall Hanging

FAFNISMOL WALL HANGING
(COLORPLATE 20)

Technique: Long-armed cross-stitch.
Materials: Penelope canvas, 10 count brown.
Guro or Anchor wool, use 1 strand.
Cut size: 66 inches x 32 inches.
Finished size: 60 inches x 26 inches.

One square on the pattern equals 2 double threads on the canvas. Find the center of the pattern with the aid of the arrows. Find the center of the canvas. Begin here. For stitches and finishing see Chapter Five. Compose the initials and date using the alphabet in the Appendix.

This design may be worked in DMC embroidery floss or Danish Flower Thread on aida, linen, or other counted thread material, leaving the background open or filling it in as desired, see Chapter Five.

backstitch	cross-stitch	GW	AW	DMC
⫽		57	377	841
	♦♦	335	164	924
	♥♥	127	412	349
	··	336	402	white
	∴∴	315	376	842
⌐	■	112	987	3371
	□□	138	358	801
	ωω	136	348	975
	φφ	118	313	725
	▲▲	332	314	971
	☆☆	338	218	890
	↑↑	58	162	806
	∂∂	360	333	970
	✳✳	122	397	451
	●●	133	268	470
fill in sky		55	167	
fill in ground		352	266	

Fafnismol Wall Hanging *(left)*

top

Fafnismol Wall Hanging *(center)*

Fafnismol Wall Hanging *(right)*

THE SNOW QUEEN WALL HANGING
(COLORPLATE 22)

Technique:	Long-armed cross-stitch.
Materials:	Penelope canvas, 10 count brown.
	Anchor wool, use 1 strand.
Cut size:	22 inches x 28 inches.
Finished size:	16 inches x 22 inches.

One square on the pattern equals 2 double threads on the penelope. Find the center of the pattern with the aid of the arrows. Find the center of the canvas. Begin here. For stitches and finishing see Chapter Five.

This design may be worked in DMC embroidery floss, Danish Flower Thread, or linen threads on linen, aida, or other counted thread materials, see Chapter Five. It also may be worked in a frieze with the East o' the Sun and West o' the Moon pattern and the Wonderful Adventures of Nils pattern.

backstitch	cross-stitch	AW	DFT	DMC
	■	987	240	3371
	⊙⊙	983	32	3041
	⁄⁄	982	27	452
	●●	981	235	453
	##　##	373	222	3045
	∴∴	892	28	819
	◢◢	188	227	806
	✴✴	67	323	224
	☆☆	429	88	3687
	■■	71	14	315
	==　==	870	235	316
	◆◆	858	99	472
	▲▲	95	232	554
	⌀⌀	504	229	928
	△△	161	27	334
	∨∨	432	227	930
	•　•	850	228	336
	＼＼	851	201	939
	◇◇	217	238	890
	◢◢	218	210	895
	s s	860	10	502
	−−	506	224	926

fill in 402

top

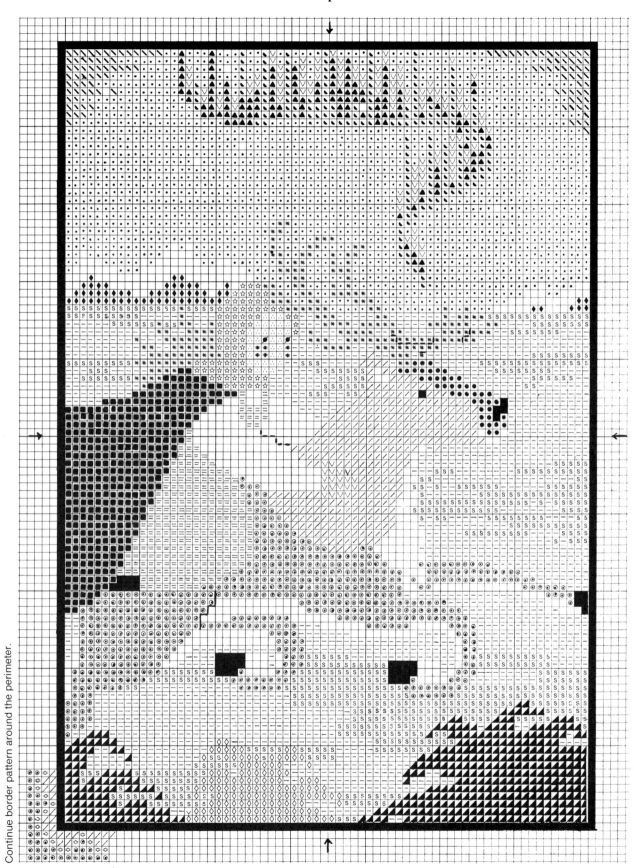

Continue border pattern around the perimeter.

The Snow Queen Wall Hanging

EAST O' THE SUN AND WEST O' THE MOON
WALL HANGING *(COLORPLATE 22)*

Technique: Sample 1, long-armed cross-stitch.
Materials: Penelope canvas, 10 count brown.
Anchor wool, use 1 strand.
Cut size: 22 inches x 28 inches.
Finished size: 16 inches x 22 inches.

Technique: Sample 2, cross-stitch.
Materials: Linen, 26 count bleached.
Danish Flower Thread, use 1
strand.
Cut size: 10 inches x 12 inches.
Finished size: 6 inches x 8 inches.

One square on the pattern equals 2 double threads on canvas, 2 threads on linen weaves and 1 square on aida weaves. Find the center of the pattern with the aid of the arrows. Find the center of the canvas or fabric. Begin here. For stitches and finishing see Chapter Five.

This design may be worked in a frieze with the Snow Queen pattern and the Wonderful Adventures of Nils pattern.

	backstitch	cross-stitch	AW	DFT	DMC
		■	987	240	3371
		★★	390	19	3033
		❘❘	895	503	3688
		♥♥	215	231	320
		##	373	222	3045
		∴∴	892	28	819
		◢◢	188	227	806
		✸✸	67	323	224
		◎◎	983	32	3041
		╱╱	982	27	452
		●●	981	235	453
		⬘⬘	504	229	928
		▲▲	161	27	334
		∨∨	432	227	930
		∶∶	850	228	336
		◥◥	851	201	939
		◪◪	218	210	895
		⬓⬓	196	203	353

fill in 402

Continue border pattern around the perimeter.

East o' the Sun and West o' the Moon Wall Hanging

THE WONDERFUL ADVENTURES OF NILS
WALL HANGING (COLORPLATE 23)

Technique: Long-armed cross-stitch.
Materials: Penelope canvas, 10 count brown.
Anchor wool, use 1 strand.
Cut size: 22 inches x 28 inches.
Finished size: 16 inches x 22 inches.

One square on the pattern equals 2 double threads on the penelope. Find the center of the pattern with the aid of the arrows. Find the center of the canvas. Begin here. For stitches and finishing see Chapter Five.

This design may be worked in DMC embroidery floss, Danish Flower Thread, or linen threads on linen, aida, or other counted thread material, see Chapter Five. It also may be worked in a frieze with the East o' the Sun and West o' the Moon pattern and the Snow Queen pattern.

	backstitch / cross-stitch	AW	DFT	DMC
	■	987	240	3371
	★★	390	19	3033
	⊚⊚	983	32	3041
	⁄⁄	982	27	452
	●●	981	235	453
	##	373	222	3045
	∴∴	892	28	819
	◢◢	188	227	806
	✦✦	67	323	224
	■■	71	14	315
	‖‖	869	3	316
	◆◆	398	32	451
	⊹⊹	504	229	928
	▲▲	161	27	334
	⋁⋁	432	227	930
	∶∶	850	228	336
	＼＼	851	201	939
	◊◊	217	238	890
	♥♥	215	231	320
	◢◢	218	210	895
	++	500	54	783
	ss	860	10	502
	==	506	224	926
	⊬⊬	216	9	367

fill in 402

Continue border pattern around the perimeter.

The Wonderful Adventures of Nils Wall Hanging

LAPP MAGIC DRUM SYMBOL
(COLORPLATE 24)

Reindeer 1

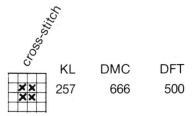

	KL	DMC	DFT
	257	666	500

Technique: Reindeer 1, long-armed cross-stitch.
Materials: Linen, 18 count bleached.
Kulört linen thread, use 1 strand.
DMC embroidery floss, use 3 or 4 strands.
Danish Flower Thread, use 2 strands.
Cut size: 23 inches x 21 inches.
Finished size: 17 inches x 15 inches.

Reindeer 2

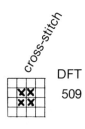

	DFT
	509

Technique: Reindeer 2, cross-stitch.
Materials: Linen, 26 count bleached.
Cut size: 14 inches x 14 inches.
Finished size: 8 inches x 8 inches.

Reindeer 3

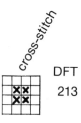

	DFT
	213

Technique: Reindeer 3, cross-stitch.
Materials: Linen, 26 count bleached.
Cut size: 14 inches x 14 inches.
Finished size: 8 inches x 8 inches.

One square on the pattern equals 2 threads on linen weaves and 1 square on aida weaves. Find the center of the pattern with the aid of the arrows. Find the center of the fabric. Begin here. For stitches and finishing see Chapter Five. See suggestions for alternate colors at the beginning of this section.

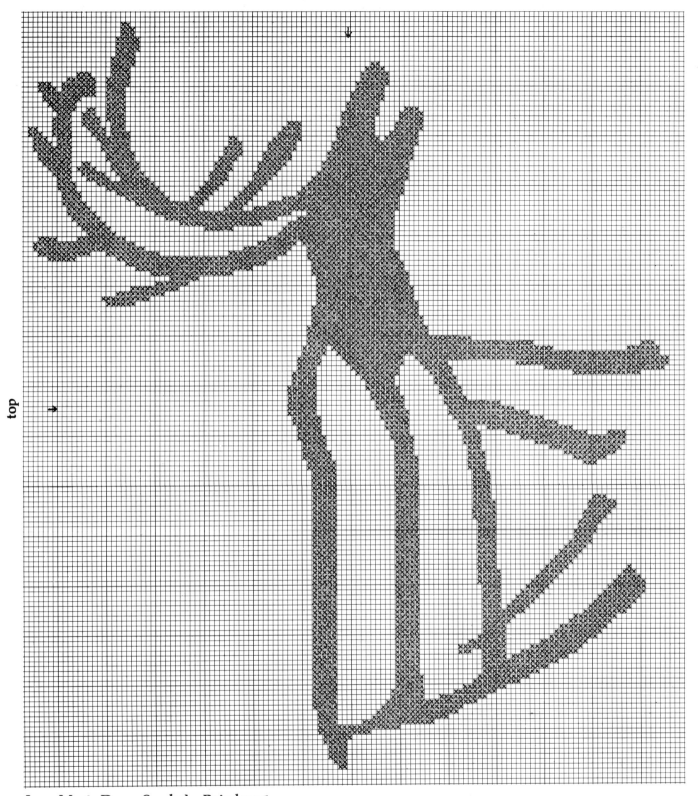

top

Lapp Magic Drum Symbol—Reindeer 1

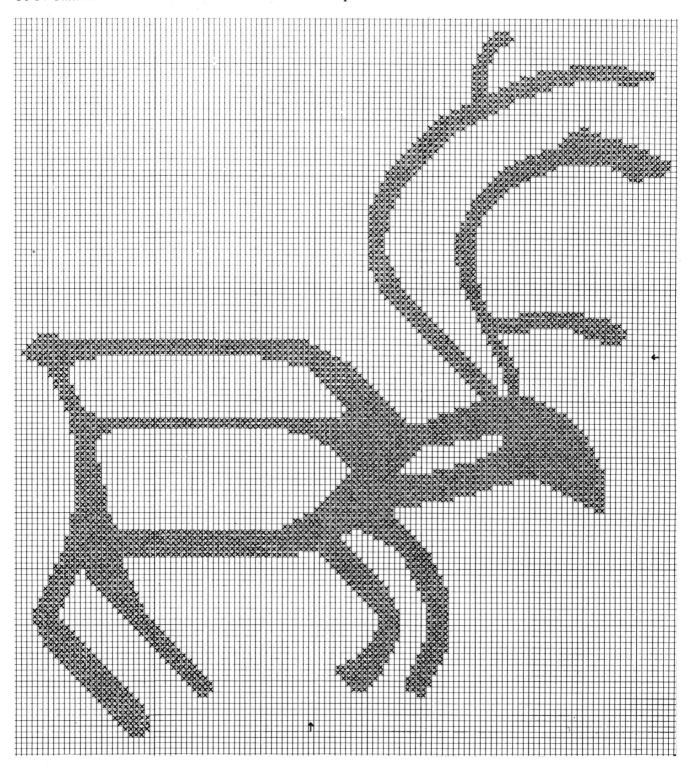

Lapp Magic Drum Symbol—Reindeer 2

top

Lapp Magic Drum Symbol—Reindeer 3

Appendix

Materials

Below are lists and charts of the embroidery threads, fabrics, and stitches used to make the samples of the patterns in this book.

THREADS

DMC = DMC divisible embroidery floss (6-ply mercerized cotton), France.

DFT = Danish Flower Thread (1-ply matte cotton), Danish Handcraft Guild, Denmark.

KL = Kulört or Klippans Lingarn (1-ply size 16/2 linen thread), Sweden.

LW = Laine separable tapisserie wool, by DMC (3-ply), France.

AW = Anchor tapisserie wool for canvas (4-ply), Great Britain.

GW = Guro embroidery yarn (3-ply, wool-viscose-acrylic blend), Norway.

Note that DMC and LW are separated to get the desired number of strands, while DFT or KL strands are combined if more than one strand is desired. AW and GW are used as is.

FABRICS

Chart 3. Fabrics used to make sample patterns in Chapter Six.

Fabric	Size	Stitches per inch
Linen	30 count	(15 stitches per inch)
	26 count	(13 stitches per inch)
	18 count	(9 stitches per inch)
Aida	14 count	(14 stitches per inch)
	11 count	(11 stitches per inch)
Linaida	15 count	(15 stitches per inch)
Salem	26-count linen weave	(13 stitches per inch)
	14-count aida weave	(14 stitches per inch)
Wool	18-count linen weave	(9 stitches per inch)
	6-count aida weave	(6 stitches per inch)
Penelope canvas	14 count	(7½ stitches per inch)
	12 count	(6 stitches per inch)
	10 count	(5 stitches per inch)
	9 count	(4½ stitches per inch)

ALTERNATIVES

Below are charts that show: suggestions for matching threads with suitable fabrics for the counted thread stitches used in this book; and how to determine the number of strands of thread for each fabric. Traditionally, linen thread and Danish Flower Thread are used only on linen grounds. Wool is used on even-weave wool fabric or canvas. Because of their nature, double cross-stitch and *gobelin* cannot be worked on aida weaves. Double cross-stitch and *gobelin* stitch are most often worked on canvas.

Chart 4. Matching stitches, threads, and fabrics.

CROSS-STITCH

Fabric	Size	Thread
Linen	30 count	DMC 2 strands / DFT 1 strand
	26 count	DMC 2 strands / DFT 1 strand
	18 count	DMC 3 strands/ DFT 2 strands / KL 1 strand / LW 1 strand
Wool	18-count linen weave	LW 1 separated strand
	6-count aida weave	LW 1 separated strand
Aida	14 count	DMC 2 strands
	11 count	DMC 3 strands
Linaida	15 count	DMC 2 strands
Salem	26-count linen weave	DMC 2 strands
	14-count aida weave	DMC 2 strands
Penelope	14 count	AW 1 strand / LW 3 strands
	12 count	AW 1 strand / GW 1 strand / LW 3 strands

LONG-ARMED CROSS-STITCH

Fabric	Size	Thread
Linen	26 count	DMC 2 strands
	18 count	KL 1 strand / LW 1 separated strand
Wool	18-count linen weave	LW 1 separated strand
Aida	14 count	DMC 2 strands
	11 count	DMC 3 strands
Salem	26-count linen weave	DMC 2 strands
	14-count aida weave	DMC 2 strands
Penelope	12 count	LW 3 strands
	10 count	AW 1 strand / GW 1 strand
	9 count	AW 1 strand / GW 1 strand

DOUBLE CROSS-STITCH

Fabric	Size	Thread
Penelope	14 count	LW 1 strand
	12 count	AW 1 strand / GW 1 strand
	10 count	AW 1 strand / GW 1 strand

UPRIGHT *GOBELIN* STITCH

Fabric	Size	Thread
Wool	18-count linen weave	LW 1 separated strand
Penelope	10 count	AW 1 strand
	9 count	AW 1 strand / GW 1 strand

Chart 5. Suggestions for matching number of threads to fabric for cross-stitch.

If the fabric holds this many stitches per inch:	Use this many strands of:				
	DMC	DFT	KL	LW/TW	AW/GW
6	4-6	2-3	1	1	1
7	4-6	2-3	1	1	1
8	4	2-3	1	1	—
9	4	2	1	1	—
10	3	2	1	—	—
11	3	2	1	—	—
12	2-3	1-2	—	—	—
13	2	1	—	—	—
14	2	1	—	—	—
15	2	1	—	—	—
18	2	1	—	—	—
20	1-2	1	—	—	—
22	1	—	—	—	—

Suppliers

Below is a list of sources of counted thread embroidery supplies. Many of them include mail order service.

Gloria's Scandinavian Gifts
11915 Park South
Tacoma, Washington 98444
(206) 537-8502

The World in Stitches Mail Order Service
82 South Street
Milford, New Hampshire 03055
(603) 673-6616

The Dove's Eye
3333 Kolstad Avenue
Duluth, Minnesota 55803

Ginnie Thompson Originals
Box 930
Pawley's Island, South Carolina 29585
(800) 845-8073

Mace & Nairn
89 Crane Street
Salisbury, Wiltshire, England

Heirloom Embroidery
9 Burnley Road
Willesden, London NW10, England

The Danish Handcraft Guild
(Haandarbejdts Fremme)
Tranevej 16-20
2400 Kobenhavn NV, Denmark

Husfliden
(Norwegian Home Arts Association)
Mollergaten 4
0179 Oslo 1, Norway

Aktiebolaget Nordiska Kompaniet
Box 7195
Stockholm, Sweden

Schweizer Heimatwerk
Industristrasse 6
CH-8305 Dietlikon, Schweiz (Switzerland)

Stadia Handcraft
85 Elizabeth Street
Paddington, N.S.W., Australia 2021

For needlework framing contact:
Art Concepts Gallery
3800½ Bridgeport Way West
Tacoma, Washington 98466
(206) 565-0822

Alphabet

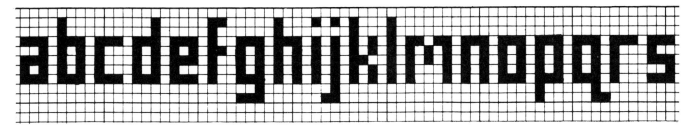

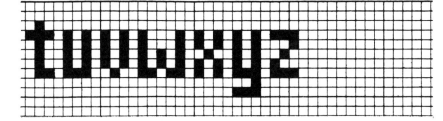

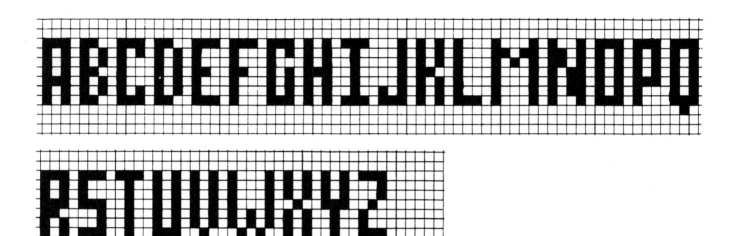

Bib Pattern

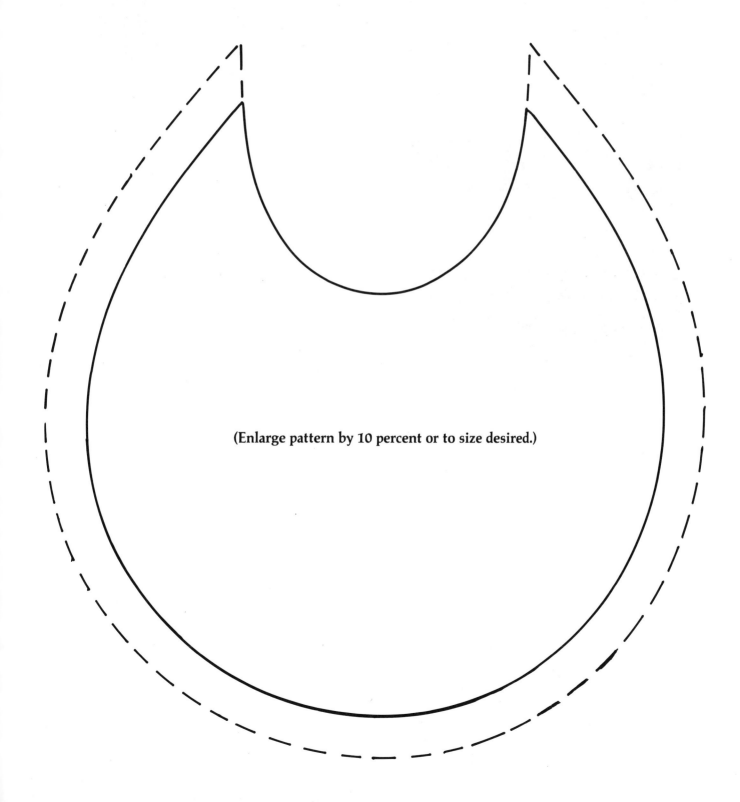

(Enlarge pattern by 10 percent or to size desired.)

Picture Frame Pattern

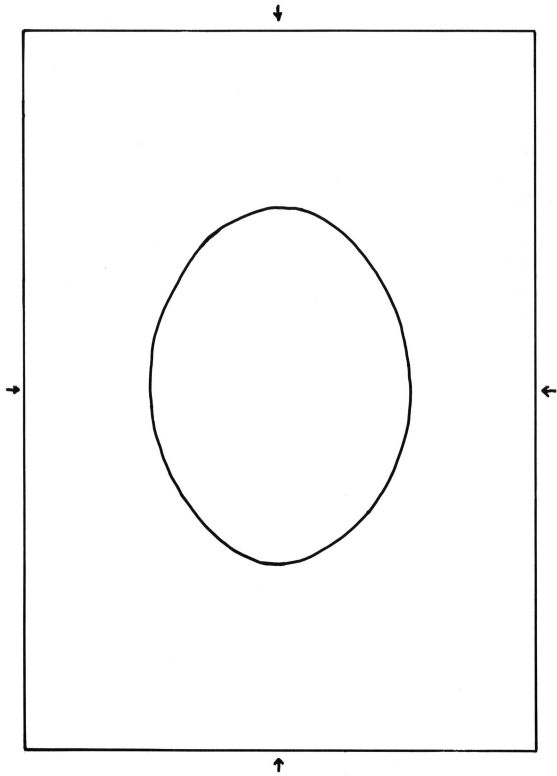

Endnotes

1. Eric Oxenstierna, *The Norsemen.* (Connecticut, 1965). Interesting speculations on Queen Asa are in Chapter 9.
2. Phyllis Ackerman, The Norse origins of the Bayeux Tapestry are discussed in detail in *Tapestry: The Mirror of Civilization.* (New York, 1970).
3. Anna-Maija Nylen, *Swedish Handcraft.* (New York, 1977), p. 166. This book is an in-depth look at the history and evolution of the handcrafts of Sweden.
4. J. R. R. Tolkien, "On Fairie Stories," *The Tolkien Reader.* (New York, 1966), p. 56. Tolkien was a student of medieval northern European literature and could read many of the Scandinavian works in the original language.
5. Frederika Blankner, (comp.), *The History of the Scandinavian Literatures.* (New York, 1938), p. 3–8. The introduction provides a discussion of the personalities of the various Scandinavian literatures.
6. From a lecture on Hans Christian Andersen given by Dr. Suzanne Rahn at Pacific Lutheran University in Tacoma, Washington, in the fall of 1984.
7. For more on the Lapp use of magic drums, see Ernest Manker's *People of Eight Seasons* or Björn Collinder's *The Lapps.*

Glossary

Aida. A cotton fabric for counted thread embroidery, woven so that it is made up of squares on which to work the embroidery.

Almue. Danish for "the common people."

Anchor yarn. An all-wool yarn for working counted thread embroidery on canvas.

Barfrøstue. On old Norwegian farms, the house or dwelling building.

Bronze Age. Period when human culture had developed to the point of using bronze tools and weapons (3500–1000 B.C.).

Bunad. Norwegian word for folk dress.

Carding. Disentangling and straightening the fibers of wool, flax, or other material so it can be spun into thread.

Counted thread embroidery. A specific type of embroidery in which identical stitches are counted out from a graph on paper forming a pattern or design.

Danish Flower Thread. A matte cotton thread that is dyed as close as possible to natural vegetable dye colors. This thread is manufactured by the Danish Handcraft Guild specifically for counted thread embroidery.

Darning. Sewing a network of stitches to repair a fabric or to make a fabric (usually a picture tapestry).

Diamondsting. Norwegian for double cross-stitch.

Distaff. A wooden staff that holds a clump of raw fiber (linen, wool, etc.) as it is hand-spun on a spindle.

District art. Folk art that developed in distinctive ways in certain regions of Scandinavia.

DMC embroidery floss. A 6-strand glossy cotton floss used for many techniques of embroidery.

Ecclesiastical. Of or pertaining to the church, specifically Christianity.

Embroidery. The art of decorating fabric using needle and thread.

Fairyfolk. Any one of many alien races believed in folklore to co-inhabit earth with human beings; some are benevolent, most are dangerous.

Flax. An annual plant with blue flowers and slender leaves; the fibers of the stem are spun to make linen.

Flettesting. Danish for long-armed cross-stitch, literally "braided stitch."

Flotedricka. A Swedish peasant drink traditionally served at the flax harvest.

Folk art. Handcrafts and art created by the peasants or common people.

Folkedragter. Danish for folk dress.

Folkdräkter. Swedish for folk costume.

Folklore. The traditional beliefs, legends, sayings, and customs of a people.

Frost giants. The ancient ancestors of the trolls; huge, strong, and enemies to the gods and the heroes.

Free embroidery. Embroidery that is not dependent on the threads of the material; stitches are worked in any direction, almost as if one were "painting" the piece.

Gamli krosssamurinn. Icelandic, literally "the old cross-stitch" or long-armed cross-stitch, which was used in Iceland before cross-stitch.

Glitsaumur. The Icelandic term for straight pattern darning. This counted thread technique preceded *gobelin.*

Gobelin. A satin-stitch embroidery worked by counting threads on the background fabric; *gobelin* worked diagonally is also known as needlepoint, but in Scandinavia *gobelin* is most often worked in upright stitches.

Guro yarn. A tapestry yarn blended of wool, viscose, and acrylic, and used for canvas embroidery.

Haltiga. In Finnish folklore a good-natured spirit who often acts as a guide for human beings.

Handcraft. The skill of making something by hand.

Homespun. Cloth spun and woven at home by peasants and common folk.

Hulderfolk. "The hidden people." In Scandinavian folklore, a race of soulless, elflike fairyfolk, dangerous to human beings.

Iconography. The art of representing figures, particularly religious figures and symbols.

Iron Age. Period when man developed the use of iron tools and weapons (1000 B.C.–A.D. 100).

Kansallispuku. Finnish for folk dress.

Kaksoisristipisto. Finnish for double cross-stitch.

Klostersøm. Norwegian for upright *gobelin* stitch.

Korssting. Danish and Norwegian for cross-stitch.

Korsstygn. Swedish name for cross-stitch.

Krosssaumurinn. Icelandic for cross-stitch.

Kulört or Klippans lingarn. Pure linen thread made in Scandinavia.

Laakapisto. Finnish for upright *gobelin* stitch.

Laid and couched embroidery. A type of free embroidery where the thread is laid on the fabric, then anchored down with couching stitches.

Laine wool. A divisible 3-ply worsted used in counted thread embroidery on even-weave wool or canvas. Made by DMC, France.

Lichens. Small plants consisting of a symbiotic coupling of fungus and algae, used for dyeing textiles.

Linen. Fabric woven from the prepared fibers of the flax plant.

Loom. The frame on which weaving takes place.

Lucia. A young woman of Sicily who gave all she owned to the poor and was martyred for her faith. Her name means "light," and her festival on 13 December celebrates the return of light after winter. She died in A.D. 304.

Madder. Northern bedstraw, a plant used to make a bright red or crimson dye.

Mangletraer. Flat wooden implements for ironing linen that were used by the peasants in Scandinavia before the twentieth century.

Middle Ages. Technically the period in European history between ancient and modern times (A.D. 476–1450). It is used in this book to refer to the years A.D. 1050–1450.

Migration Period. Period in Europe when tribes inhabiting the continent were nomadic and migratory and followed the herds of animals they hunted. (A.D. 200–800).

Mordant. A substance used in dyeing fabric to fix the dye to the cloth and prevent it from washing out.

Narrative textile. Any textile that illustrates a story or shows a picture by means of embroidered or woven-in figures or words.

Navneduker. Norwegian, literally "name rags" or samplers embroidered with a sampling of stitches or figures.

Navnklude. Danish for "name rags" or samplers.

Nisse. A temperamental, solitary hobgoblin, who makes his home in a barn, where he watches over the farm animals; if well-treated he gives prosperity, if not he may cause calamity then find a new barn.

Norse Code. The code of honor and ethics evolved and adhered to by the Vikings.

Odin. The chief diety in Norse mythology, god of art, war, and the dead.

Penelope canvas. A sturdy, heavy canvas on which counted thread embroidery can be worked in wool.

Ragnarok. In Norse mythology, the great battle between the gods and heroes and the frost giants, which will take place at the end of the world.

Retting. Soaking flax in water to cause partial rotting so the fibers can be separated from the woody parts.

Ristipisto. Finnish for cross-stitch.

Saeter. Lodgings high up in the Norwegian mountains, where young farm girls took the cattle to graze in the summertime.

Saga. A medieval Scandinavian story of history, legend, or local happenings.

Salem cloth. A synthetic counted thread fabric, which comes in both a linen weave and an aida weave.

Serger. A machine for overcasting edges of fabric to prevent raveling.

Skalds. The ancient Scandinavian poets of the Viking Age.

Smyrna. The term used in both Denmark and Sweden for double cross-stitch.

Spindle. A rounded wooden rod on which fibers are spun into thread by hand.

Spinning wheel. A machine with a spindle driven by a large wheel worked by foot or hand. It is used for spinning fibers into thread.

Sprang. Embroidery made by braiding threads with sticks.

Stabbur. Loft house. A storage building used for grain and vegetables on Norwegian farms.

Symbolism. The representation of ideas or things with symbols, as the cross symbolizes the church, or the sun symbolizes light.

Tabby weave. A striped weave.

Tapestry. Technically used only for woven wall hangings, but sometimes used in reference to embroidery, such as the Bayeux Tapestry.

Tapestry needle. A blunt needle with a large eye made specifically for counted thread embroidery.

Tjaldr. The Old Norse word, literally "tent decorations," for the custom of hanging the inside of homes with fabrics and textiles.

Tomten. Swedish word for *nisse.*

Trolls. Large, ugly, dirty, extremely stupid creatures of the darkness in Scandinavian folklore, who work evil, cast spells, and hoard treasure in their caves. Unable to abide light, they turn to stone at the sight of the sun.

Tvist **or** *tvistur.* The name for the fabric on which long-armed cross-stitch was first worked in Scandinavia.

Tvistsöm. Swedish term for long-armed cross-stitch.

Twistsøm. Norwegian for long-armed cross-stitch.

Upphlutur. The name of the everyday costume for women in Iceland.

Valhalla. The great mythological hall where Odin receives the fallen warriors.

Valkyries. The three handmaidens of Odin, according to Norse mythology.

Vied. A plant used for making blue textile dye.

Vikings. Scandinavian sailors who roamed the seas and pirated along the coast of Europe from A.D. 800–1050.

Viking Age. That period in Scandinavian history when the Vikings were active (A.D. 800–1050).

Weaving. The making of fabric on a loom.

Woad. A plant of the mustard family that is used to make blue fabric dyes.

Wool. Yarn spun from the fibers of sheep fleece.

Yggdrasil. In Norse mythology, the giant ash tree at the center of the universe, which spread out and held the nine Norse worlds.

Yule. Christmastime in Scandinavia.

Bibliography

Scandinavian Textiles and Folk Arts

Almgren, Bertil, et al. *The Viking.* Gothenburg, Sweden: A. B. Nordbok, 1975.

Anker, Peter. *Norsk folkekunst.* Oslo: J. W. Cappelens Forlag AS, 1975.

Bengtsson, Gerda. *Cross-Stitch Patterns in Color.* New York: Van Nostrand Reinhold Co., 1974.

Collinder, Björn. *The Lapps.* New York: The American-Scandinavian Foundation, 1949.

Danish Handcraft Guild. *Contemporary Danish Cross-Stitch Design.* New York: Hastings House Publisher, 1982.

_____. *Counted Cross-Stitch Designs for Christmas.* New York: Charles Scribner's Sons, 1976.

deDillmont, Thérèse. *Lapland Embroidery.* Mulhouse, France: DMC Library, 1978.

Engelstad, Helen. "Norwegian Art Weaving." In *Native Art of Norway,* edited by Roar Hauglid. New York: Frederick A. Praeger, 1967.

Gilbertson, Donald E., and James F. Richards. *A Treasury of Norwegian Folk-Art.* Wisconsin: Tin Chicken. 1975.

Graham-Campbell, James. *The Viking World.* New York: Ticknor & Fields, 1980.

Gudjónsson, Elsa E. *Traditional Icelandic Embroidery.* Reykjavik, Iceland: Iceland Review, 1985.

Hald, Arthur, and Sven Erik Skawonius. *Contemporary Swedish Design.* Stockholm: Nordisk Rotogravyr, 1951.

Hansen, H. J., editor. *European Folk Art in Europe and the Americas.* New York: McGraw-Hill, 1968.

Hauglid, Roar. *Norway: A Thousand Years of Native Arts and Crafts.* Oslo: Mittet & Co. A/S, 1956.

Manker, Ernst. *People of Eight Seasons: The Story of the Lapps.* New York: The Viking Press, 1964.

Makkila, Katri, and Maija-Leena Seppala. *Vanha suoma lainen pistokirjonta.* Helsinki: Werner Soderstrom Osakeyhtio, 1980.

McFadden, David Revere, editor. *Scandinavian Modern Design 1880–1980.* New York: Harry N. Abrams, 1982.

Nielsen, Edith. *Scandinavian Embroidery Past and Present.* New York: Charles Scribner's Sons, 1978.

Nordman, C.A. *Finlands Medeltida Konsthantverk: Arts and Crafts in Medieval Finland.* Helsingfors, Finland: Museiverket, 1980.

Norwegian Tapestries. An exhibit sponsored by the Government of Norway and circulated by The Smithsonian Institute, 1959–60.

Nylen, Anna-Maja. *Swedish Handcrafts.* Translated by Anne-Charlotte Hanes Harvey. New York: Van Nostrand Reinhold Co., 1977.

Oxenstierna, Eric. *The Norsemen.* Greenwich, Conn.: New York Graphic Society Publishing Ltd., 1965.

Phaidon Press. *The Bayeux Tapestry: A Comprehensive Survey.* London: Phaidon Press, 1965.

Plath, Iona. *The Decorative Arts of Sweden.* New York: Dover, 1966.

Rajanen, Aini. *Of Finnish Ways.* Minneapolis: Dillon Press, Inc., 1981.

Roalson, Louise. *Notably Norwegian.* Decorah, Iowa: The Norwegian-American Museum, 1982.

Stalder, Valerie. *Lapland.* Vol. 26 of *This Beautiful World Series.* Palo Alto, California: Kodansha International Ltd., 1971.

Sterner, Maj. *Homecrafts in Sweden.* Stockholm: Fritzeskungl Hovebokhandel, 1939.

Stewart, Janice. *The Folk Arts of Norway.* New York: Dover, 1972.

Swedish Handcraft Society. *Counted Cross-Stitch Patterns and Designs.* New York: Charles Scribner's Sons, 1976.

Wandel, Gertie. *Klassiske Korssting.* Copenhagen: Politikens Forlag, 1971.

Textiles and Folk Arts in General

Ackerman, Phyllis. *Tapestry: The Mirror of Civilization.* New York: AMS Press, Inc., 1970.

Ames, Kenneth L. *Beyond Necessity: Art in the Folk Tradition.* Delaware: The Winterthur Museum, 1977.

Coats, J. and P., Ltd. *100 Embroidery Stitches.* East Kilbride, England: Thomson Litho, Ltd., 1981.

Collingwood, Peter. *The Techniques of Sprang: Plaiting on Stretched Threads.* London: Faber and Faber, 1974.

deDillmont, Thérèse. *The Complete Encyclopedia of Needlework.* 2d. Ed. Philadelphia: Running Press, 1978.

Furry, Margaret S., and Bess M. Viemont. *Home Dyeing with Natural Dyes.* Washington, D.C.: U.S. Department of Agriculture, 1935.

Gostelow, Mary. *The Complete International Book of Embroidery.* New York: Simon & Schuster, 1977.

————. *A World of Embroidery.* New York: Charles Scribner's Sons, 1975.

Spiers, Gill, and Sigrid Quemby. *A Treasury of Embroidery Designs: Charts and Patterns from the Great Collections.* London: Bell and Hyman Ltd., 1985.

Symonds, Mary, and Louise Preece. *Needlework Through the Ages.* London: Hodder & Stoughton, Ltd., 1928.

Thomson, Francis Paul. *Tapestry, Mirror of Civilization.* New York: Crown Publishers, Inc., 1980.

Scandinavian Folk Costumes

Berg, Inga Arno, and Gunnel Hazelius Berg. *Folk Costumes of Sweden—A Living Tradition.* Vasteras, Sweden: ICA Bokforlag, 1975.

Gudjónsson, Elsa E. *The National Costume of Women in Iceland.* Reykjavik, Iceland: LITBRA-offset, 1970.

Kragelund, Minna. *Folkedragter.* Copenhagen: Lademann.

Nylen, Anna-Maja. *Folkdräkter.* Stockholm: Nordiska Museet, 1949.

Oy, Helmi Vuorelma. *Kansallispukuja.* Lahti, Finland: Esan Kirjapaino Oy, 1985.

Skavhaug, Kjirsti. *Norwegian Bunads.* Oslo: Hjemmenes Forlag, 1982.

Stewart, Janice. *The Folk Arts of Norway.* New York: Dover, 1972.

The National Museum of Finland. *Folk Costumes and Textiles.* Helsinki: Government Printing Center, 1982.

Tratteberg, Gunvor Ingstad. "Folk-costume." In *Native Art of Norway,* edited by Roar Hauglid. New York: Frederick A. Praeger, 1967.

Woxholth, Yngve. *Vare vakre bunader.* Oslo: Hjemmenes Forlag, 1969.

Scandinavian Folk Literature and Related Books

Andersen, Hans Christian. *Fairy Tales.* New York: The Viking Press, 1981.

Andersen, Hans Christian. *The True Story of My Life.* Translated by Mary Howitt. New York: The American-Scandinavian Foundation, 1926.

Anderson, George K., trans. *The Saga of the Völsungs.* Newark, New Jersey: Associated University Presses, Inc., 1982.

Asbjørnsen, Peter Christian, and Jørgen Moe. *Norwegian Folktales.* New York: Pantheon Books, 1960.

d'Aulaire, Ingri, and Edgar d'Aulaire. *d'Aulaires' Trolls.* New York: Doubleday and Co., Inc., 1972.

Bellows, Henry Adams, trans. *The Poetic Edda.* New York: The American-Scandinavian Foundation, 1968.

Blankner, Frederika, comp. *The History of the Scandinavian Literatures.* New York: Dial Press, Inc., 1938.

Booss, Claire, ed. *Scandinavian Folk & Fairytales.* New York: Avenel Books, 1984.

Bowman, James C., and Margery Bianco. *Tales From a Finnish Tupa.* Chicago: Albert Whitman & Co., 1970.

Bredsdorff, Elias. *Hans Christian Andersen: The Story of His Life and Work 1805–1875.* New York: Charles Scribner's Sons, 1975.

Briggs, K. M. *The Fairies in Tradition and Literature.* London: Routledge & Kegan Paul, 1967.

Bringsvaerd, Tor Age. *Phantoms and Fairies from Norwegian Folklore.* Translated by Pat Shaw Iversen. Oslo: Johan Grundt Tanum Forlag, 1970.

Craigie, William A. *The Icelandic Sagas.* London: Cambridge University Press, 1913.

Craigie, William A., trans. *Scandinavian Folk-Lore.* Detroit: Singing Tree Press, 1970.

Crossley-Holland, Kevin. *The Norse Myths.* New York: Pantheon, 1980.

Dascent, George Webbe, trans. *East o' the Sun and West o' the Moon.* New York: Dover, 1970.

Davidson, H. R. Ellis. *Scandinavian Mythology.* London: Paul Hamlyn, 1969.

Ibsen, Henrik. *Peer Gynt.* Translated by Rolf Fjelde. Minneapolis: University of Minnesota Press, 1980.

Keary, A., and E. Keary. *The Heroes of Asgard.* New York: Mayflower Books, 1979.

Keightley, Thomas. *The World Guide to Gnomes, Fairies, Elves and Other Little People.* New York: Avenel, 1978.

Lagerlöf, Selma. *The Wonderful Adventures of Nils.* New York: Grosset & Dunlap, 1907.

Lewis, Naomi, ed. *Hans Andersen's Fairytales.* Middlesex, England: Puffin Books, 1981.

Lindow, John. *Swedish Legends and Folktales.* Berkeley: University of California Press, 1978.

Lonnrot, Elias. *Kalevala.* Translated by Francis Peabody

Mougin, Jr. Cambridge: Harvard University Press, 1963.

Olenius, Elsa, ed. *Great Swedish Fairytales.* New York: Dell, 1973.

Olrik, Axel. *A Book of Danish Ballads.* New York: American-Scandinavian Foundation, 1939.

Raffel, Burton, trans. *Beowulf.* New York: The New American Library, 1963.

Simpson, Jacquelin. *Icelandic Folktales and Legends.* Berkeley: University of California Press, 1972.

Sturlusson, Snorri. *Heimskringla, History of the Kings of Norway.* Austin: The American-Scandinavian Foundation, 1964.

————. *The Prose Edda.* Translated by Arthur Gilchrist Brodeur. New York: The American-Scandinavian Foundation, 1929.

Tolkien, J. R. R. *The Hobbit.* New York: Ballantine Books, 1937.

————. *The Lord of the Rings.* New York: Ballantine Books, 1956.

————. "On Fairy Stories." In *The Tolkien Reader.* New York: Ballantine Books, 1937.

Topelius, Zacharias. *Canute Whistlewinks and Other Stories.* Translated by C. W. Foss. Chicago: E. M. Hale, 1927.

Undset, Sigrid. *Kristin Lavransdatter.* New York: Alfred A. Knopf, 1923.

Fox, Matthew. *Original Blessing.* Santa Fe, New Mexico: Bear & Co., Inc., 1983.

Hulme, F. Edward. *The History, Principles and Practices of Symbolism in Christian Art.* London: Swan Sonnenschein, 1891.

Jung, Carl Gustav. *Man and His Symbols.* New York: Doubleday & Co., Inc., 1964.

————. *Memories, Dreams, Reflections.* New York: Random House, 1965.

————. *Psyche & Symbol.* New York: Doubleday & Co., Inc., 1958.

Kelsey, Morton T. *The Other Side of Silence.* New York: Paulist Press, 1976.

LeGuin, Ursula K. *The Language of the Night.* New York: Berkeley Books, 1979.

Richards, Glyn. *The Philosophy of Gandhi.* London: Curson Press Ltd., 1982.

Richards, Mary C. *Centering.* Connecticut: Wesleyan University Press, 1962.

Symbols and Centering

Appleton, LeRoy H., and Stephen Bridges. *Symbolism in Liturgical Art.* New York: Charles Scribner's Sons, 1959.

Auel, Jean. *Clan of the Cave Bear.* New York: Bantam Books, 1981.

Cirlot, J. E. *A Dictionary of Symbols.* London: Routledge & Kegan Paul, 1962.

Edinger, Edward F. *Ego and Archetype.* Baltimore: Penguin Books Inc., 1972.

Eliade, Mircea. *Images and Symbols.* New York: Sheed and Ward, 1969.

————. *The Sacred and the Profane.* New York: Harper & Brothers, 1957.

————. *Shamanism.* New Jersey: Princeton University Press, 1964.

Ferguson, George. *Signs and Symbols in Christian Art.* New York: Oxford University Press, 1954.

Index

OTHER BOOKS
FROM PACIFIC SEARCH PRESS

COOKING

American Wood Heat Cookery (2d Ed. Revised & Enlarged) by Margaret Byrd Adams

The Apple Cookbook by Kyle D. Fulwiler

The Bean Cookbook: Dry Legume Cookery by Norma S. Upson

The Berry Cookbook (2d Ed. Revised & Enlarged) by Kyle D. Fulwiler

Canning and Preserving without Sugar (Updated) by Norma M. MacRae, R.D.

The Eating Well Cookbook by John Doerper

Eating Well: A Guide to Foods of the Pacific Northwest by John Doerper

The Eggplant Cookbook by Norma S. Upson

A Fish Feast by Charlotte Wright

Food 101: A Student Guide to Quick and Easy Cooking by Cathy Smith

Kayak Cookery: A Handbook of Provisions and Recipes by Linda Daniel

One Potato, Two Potato: A Cookbook by Constance Bollen and Marlene Blessing

River Runners' Recipes by Patricia Chambers

The Salmon Cookbook (2d Ed.) by Jerry Dennon

Shellfish Cookery: Absolutely Delicious Recipes from the West Coast by John Doerper

Starchild & Holahan's Seafood Cookbook by Adam Starchild and James Holahan

Wild Mushroom Recipes by Puget Sound Mycological Society

The Zucchini Cookbook (3rd Ed. Revised & Enlarged) by Paula Simmons

CRAFTS

The Chilkat Dancing Blanket by Cheryl Samuel

The Guide to Successful Tapestry Weaving by Nancy Harvey

An Illustrated Guide to Making Oriental Rugs by Gordon W. Scott

Patterns for Tapestry Weaving: Projects and Techniques by Nancy Harvey

Spinning and Weaving with Wool (Updated) by Paula Simmons

HEALTH

A Practical Guide to Independent Living for Older People by Alice H. Phillips and Caryl K. Roman

NATURE

The Birdhouse Book: Building Houses, Feeders, and Baths by Don McNeil

Growing Organic Vegetables West of the Cascades by Steve Solomon

Marine Mammals of Eastern North Pacific and Arctic Waters (2d Ed. Revised) edited by Delphine Haley

Photographing the North American West: How and Where to Capture Nature on Film by Erwin and Peggy Bauer

Seabirds of Eastern North Pacific and Arctic Waters edited by Delphine Haley

NORTHWEST SCENE

At the Forest's Edge: Memoir of a Physician-Naturalist by David Tirrell Hellyer

The Pike Place Market: People, Politics, and Produce by Alice Shorett and Murray Morgan

Seattle Photography by David Barnes

The Seattle GuideBook (6th Ed. Revised & Enlarged) by Archie Satterfield

They Tried to Cut It All by Edwin Van Syckle

OUTDOOR RECREATION

Cross-Country Downhill and Other Nordic Mountain Skiing Techniques (3d Ed. Revised & Enlarged) by Steve Barnett

The Coastal Kayaker: Kayak Camping on the Alaska and B.C. Coast by Randel Washburne

Derek C. Hutchinson's Guide to Sea Kayaking by Derek C. Hutchinson

Fundamentals of Kayak Navigation by David Burch

Kayak Trips in Puget Sound and the San Juan Islands by Randel Washburne

River Runners' Recipes by Patricia Chambers

The White-Water River Book: A Guide to Techniques, Equipment, Camping, and Safety by Ron Watters/Robert Winslow, photography

Whitewater Trips for Kayakers, Canoeists and Rafters in British Columbia, Greater Vancouver through Whistler and Thompson River Regions by Betty Pratt-Johnson

Whitewater Trips for Kayakers, Canoeists and Rafters on Vancouver Island by Betty Pratt-Johnson

TRAVEL

Alaska's Backcountry Hideaways: Southcentral by Roberta L. Graham

Alaska's Southeast: Touring the Inside Passage (2d Ed. Revised & Enlarged) by Sarah Eppenbach

The Bed-and-Breakfast Traveler: Touring the West Coast by Lewis Green

Camping Alaska and Canada's Yukon: The Motorist's Handbook to North Country Campgrounds and Roadways by Mike and Marilyn Miller

Cruising the Columbia and Snake Rivers (2d Ed. Revised & Enlarged) by Sharlene P. and Ted W. Nelson and Joan LeMieux

Cruising the Pacific Coast, Acapulco to Skagway (4th Ed. Revised) by Carolyn and Jack West

The Getaway Guide I: Short Vacations in the Pacific Northwest (2d Ed. Revised & Enlarged) by Marni and Jake Rankin

The Getaway Guide II: More Short Vacations in the Pacific Northwest (2d Ed. Revised & Enlarged) by Marni and Jake Rankin

The Getaway Guide III: Short Vacations in Northern California by Marni and Jake Rankin

The Getaway Guide IV: Short Vacations in Southern California by Marni and Jake Rankin

Journey to the High Southwest: A Traveler's Guide (2d Ed. Revised) by Robert Casey